Slavery to Integration
Black Americans in West Texas

edited by
Bruce A. Glasrud and Paul H. Carlson

with
Tai D. Kreidler

Slavery to Integration
Black Americans in West Texas

edited by
Bruce A. Glasrud and Paul H. Carlson

with
Tai D. Kreidler

McMurry University
Abilene, Texas

Library of Congress Cataloging-in-Publication Data

Slavery to integration: Black Americans in West Texas / edited by
Bruce A. Glasrud and Paul H. Carlson ; with Tai D. Kreidler.
  p. cm.
Includes bibliographical references.
ISBN-13: 978-1-933337-26-5 (pbk.: alk. paper)
ISBN-10: 1-933337-26-5 (pbk.: alk. paper)
  1. African Americans—Texas, West—History. 2. African Americans—Texas, West—Social conditions. 3. African Americans—Texas, West—Biography. 4. Texas, West—Race relations. 5. Texas, West—Social conditions. 6. Texas, West—Biography. I. Glasrud, Bruce A. II. Carlson, Paul Howard. III. Kreidler, Tai D.

E185.93.T4S49 2007
976.40496073—dc22

2007028522

Copyright 2007, State House Press
All Rights Reserved

State House Press
McMurry Station, Box 637
Abilene, TX 79697-0637
(325) 572-3974
(325) 572-3991 fax
www.mcwhiney.org/press

No part of this book may be reproduced without written permission from
State House Press, unless by reviewers for reviews.

Printed in the United States of America

Distributed by Texas A&M University Press Consortium
1-800-826-8911 • www.tamu.edu/upress

ISBN-10: 1-933337-26-5
ISBN-13: 978-1-933337-26-5
10 9 8 7 6 5 4 3 2 1

Book Designed by Rosenbohm Graphic Design

*For B.W. Aston and in memory of
Rupert Norval Richardson*

TABLE OF CONTENTS

Preface   9

Introduction
Black Americans in West Texas   13
Paul H. Carlson and Bruce A. Glasrud

Articles
Black and Mexican Slaves in Young County, Texas, 1856-1865   27
Barbara A. Ledbetter

D.W. Wallace ("80 John"): An African American Cattleman on the Texas Frontier   31
R.C. Crane

Nig London: Throckmorton County Cowman   38
Lawrence Clayton

William R. Shafter Commanding Black Troops in West Texas   44
Paul H. Carlson

Second Lieutenant Henry O. Flipper: A Black Officer on the West Texas Frontier   58
Donald R. McClung

Blacks in San Angelo: Relations Between Fort Concho and the City, 1875-1889   72
Patricia E. Gower

The Lost Treaty of the Black Seminoles   84
Eric Emmerson Strong

Abilene's Minority Population and the 1900 Census   98
Karen Turner

Black Lubbock   106
Robert L. Foster and Alwyn Barr

Edward Struggs and Mae Simmons: Two African American Educators and the Provisions for Black Schools in Lubbock, Texas, 1930-1970   119
June M. Steele

The Beginnings of Integration in San Angelo I.S.D.   131
Gregory A. Doherty

Desegregation in West Texas: *The United States v. Ector County I.S.D.* Case   140
Bryan L. Smith

Contributors   156

Bibliography
Year Book Articles on African Americans   159

Index   163

PREFACE

Black Americans first arrived in West Texas in the early sixteenth century. They came to the region attached to Spanish exploring parties. Later, they came to other parts of Texas as runaway slaves, adventurers, and mustangers. Slave owners brought some black Americans to Texas, and in the year 1800 or so, perhaps one thousand African Americans lived in Texas. The black American presence in Texas grew in the days after Mexico secured its independence from Spain in 1821, and about the time of the Civil War blacks moved again into West Texas. Once freed from slavery, many blacks arrived in West Texas as cowboys; a few became cattlemen. They took to other occupations as well, and after the turn of the twentieth century their numbers in West Texas increased significantly, reaching in places to nearly ten percent of the population.

Most blacks in West Texas lived in small towns and in rural areas. Too often they were illiterate or scarcely educated and extremely poor, suggesting perhaps the inadequacy of rigidly segregated school systems, the low state per pupil expenditures for blacks, and the difficulty of regular or long attendance. Oftentimes such terrorist organizations as the Ku Klux Klan prevented educational improvement. Whatever the cause, black illiteracy neared 48 percent in the greater South in 1900; white illiteracy, by comparison was 12 percent at the time.

Fortunately, the level of educational achievement of black Americans improved; by 1930 illiteracy had dropped to 27 percent. The NAACP and the Urban League, both of which worked to improve job and educational opportunities, get some credit for the positive change. In the 1930s Franklin D. Roosevelt's New Deal legislation, such as minimum wage, social security, unemployment insurance, and the various work and training programs, aided all African Americans, and in West Texas the New Deal's agricultural programs were most significant.

During the 1940s the influence of World War II encouraged black migration to West Texas. African Americans entered the region to take advantage of farm-related jobs, to work at the new air bases springing up in Lubbock, San Angelo, Amarillo, and elsewhere. Jobs in the oil and gas fields and in growing urban communities kept the new arrivals in West Texas afterward, and encouraged additional black migration as the century neared its end.

In 2007, black Americans in West Texas are entrepreneurs, doctors, lawyers, day laborers, educators, businessmen, preachers, farmers and ranchers, parents, scientists, nurses, and technicians. They are truck drivers, artists, craftsman, musicians, bartenders, wait persons, and barbers, and they hold a variety of other positions as well, such as teachers, professors, and administrators.

Despite a presence of some five centuries in the region, a compact history of black Americans in West Texas has not been published. No synthesis, no general study has appeared. A significant body of scholarly work on African Americans in the region exists in the form of journal articles, and some books cover specific aspects of the black experience in West Texas.

This book, then, is an attempt to fill an important gap in black studies. The editors selected twelve articles from the *West Texas Historical Association Year Book* to compile into a book. They chose the essays to cover the basic themes, topics, and issues related to the history of black Americans in West Texas, and they placed the articles in roughly a chronological order. In addition, they based their selections on each essay's readability, scholarship, and general interest for the collection.

The book is designed for a broader reading public. We believe, too, that students and scholars of Texas and Southwestern history, of African Americans, of minority studies, and of the American West in general will benefit significantly from the collection of lively articles that make up this little volume.

For help on the book we wish to thank a number of people. Without the authors, of course, the book would have been impossible. We are grateful for their cooperation and support. Several members of the West Texas Historical Association suggested articles, and staff members in the Southwest Collection at Texas Tech University helped to make the essays available. We especially thank the West Texas Historical Association for granting us permission to use the twelve articles found in *Slavery to Integration*. Carlyn E. Kahl of State House Press suggested the title, provided enthusiastic encouragement, and saw the work from manuscript to book.

                        Bruce A. Glasrud
                        Paul H. Carlson
                        Tai D. Kreidler

Introduction

Black Americans in West Texas

Paul H. Carlson and Bruce A. Glasrud

Britton "Britt" Johnson, called "Nigger Britt" by his teamster friends and known as "Black Fox" among the Kiowas, lived a life that seemed to reach from slavery to freedom and ultimately to integration. Born a slave in Tennessee about 1840, Johnson grew up on the Peters colony ranch of Moses (or Allen) Johnson. Later, Britt became something of a foreman on his owner's ranch in the Elm Creek Valley of western Young County, Texas. Here, over the years, he learned to read and write as well as to handle some basic math skills. As foreman, he enjoyed a freedom of movement not often permitted slaves, and in addition, Moses allowed Britt to raise his own horses and cattle. Britt married and he and his wife Mary, also a slave, had three children: a son, Jim, and two younger daughters.

Britt Johnson was often gone from the ranch headquarters, hauling freight, attending cattle, or moving horses. During one such absence with Judge H.D. Williams to Weatherford, on October 13, 1864, several hundred Kiowa and Comanche warriors, led by Comanche chief Little Buffalo, swooped down along Elm Creek northwest of Fort Belknap and struck several ranch homes while looking for cattle and horses. In what has become known as the Elm Creek Raid, the warriors stole livestock, killed seven ranch folks, including Britt's son Jim, and captured seven people, including Britt's wife and two daughters.

It was a grisly raid. Besides the dead and captured, at least three survivors suffered wounds during the attacks. Five Confederate soldiers, who had ridden to rescue the beleaguered ranch folks, died in their efforts, and several others received wounds. The Kiowas and Comanches, who had escaped with the seven captives and hundreds of horses and cattle, themselves suffered about twenty dead and a large number of wounded.[1]

Heart-broken, Britt Johnson lost all he valued in the raid. Nonetheless he worked to rebuild the ranch and to help stabilize the community. Then, to search for the seven captives, he asked Moses Johnson to release him from slavery, and upon being granted his freedom, Britt left Young County.

What happened next is largely conjecture and speculation. Some writers contend Johnson in January 1865 headed west to the Llano Estacado, the ranging tableland on which people of at least one Comanche division could camp free from Anglo retaliation. Others claim that Johnson moved north across the Red River seeking the captives among the people of another Comanche group and among the Kiowas.

In either case, Johnson spent a good portion of the spring and summer of 1865 searching for Mary and his two daughters plus the other captives, Elizabeth Ann FitzPatrick, her thirteen-year-old son Joseph (or E.G.), and her two granddaughters, five-year-old Charlotte ("Lottie") and two-year-old Mildred ("Milly"). The Indians killed Elizabeth's son shortly after the raid, and reportedly Milly froze to death in the camp of Comanche Chief Iron Mountain. Lottie spent nine months among the Comanches who tattooed her arms and forehead before they released her.[2]

Introduction

In the meantime, Johnson sought the captives widely and with desperation. He moved from one Comanche division to another, visiting smaller hunting groups in their favorite camping sites. He rode across the western half of Indian Territory (Oklahoma), seeking Comanche hunting bands in the upper Red and Canadian river valleys and their tributaries, and he followed the rivers into the Texas Panhandle. He moved south from there to search the Llano Estacado at Punta de Agua (Point of Water), Casas Amarillas (Yellow Houses), and Laguna Plata (Silver Lake), all important camping sites and comanchero trading centers along La Pista de Agua (Trail of Living Water). He stopped at several federal military posts along the western edge of settlement in Texas where he made inquires and sought information. The popular 1956 movie *The Searchers* starring John Wayne was roughly based on Britt Johnson's quest for his family.

Johnson got his family back. Having camped and traveled with various Comanche bands, Johnson not only learned their language and their ways of life but he became well-known, and apparently popular, among some Comanche people. Partly, as a result, or so the stories go, Asa-Havey, a Comanche chief who in 1865 was trying to improve relations with federal authorities, paid a ransom to the Comanche warriors who held Mary Johnson and her two daughters and in June returned the three black captives to a government Indian agent. In addition, United States troops under General J.L. Leavenworth in November rescued Mrs. FitzPatrick from the camp of Kiowa chief Sun Boy in northwestern Kansas.

After the return of his wife and daughters, Britt Johnson moved his family to Parker County. He settled near Weatherford and became a freighter. Over the next six years he hauled goods between Weatherford and various western forts: first to Fort Belknap in Young County and later, as the army opened them, to Fort Richardson in Jack County and Fort Griffin in northern Shackelford County.

Now a black entrepreneur, Johnson prospered. As indicated, he probably knew how to read and at least to a minimum degree how to write and perform various math skills. With the help of his wife, the powerfully built and resourceful twenty-six-year-old leader again raised a few horses and cattle on his home place, and his freighting business grew. He bought additional wagons, secured extra draft horses and mules, and hired teamsters.

Then, suddenly, in 1871, the dynamic young businessman died. On January 24 about twenty-five Kiowa warriors attacked Johnson's train of three wagons, four miles east of Salt Creek in Young County. Johnson and his two black teamsters defended themselves as best they could, but the Indian warriors overwhelmed them, killing the three freighters and mutilating their bodies. Shortly afterward, teamsters from another wagon train found and buried the dead men. The teamsters counted 173 rifle and pistol shells in the area where Johnson, protected by the dead body of his horse, had attempted to hold off the Kiowa attackers.[3]

If informants of Kenneth Neighbors, a historian who taught for many years at Midwestern State University, are correct, the Kiowas emasculated the dead black teamster. Then, they stuffed his genitals in his mouth, cut open his stomach, and placed his slain dog inside. As they rode away, the warriors discarded the scalp locks they had taken.[4]

Britt Johnson, an enterprising black freighter and businessman, learned while still a slave at least the elements of reading and writing. Unlike many black Americans he obtained his freedom before the end of the Civil War and he used a combination of responsibilities associated with his time as a slave and experiences gained in seeking his family after the war to build a respectable business integrated into the larger white world.

In 1972, Matt Braun, acknowledging Britt's remarkable story, wrote about Johnson in the introduction to his novel *Black Fox*, saying "Possibly even more astounding than the tale itself is the fact that this black man's singular exploits have remained nothing more than a footnote to history for over a century."[5] Indeed, Britt Johnson's story is exceptional, it is centered in West Texas, and it is bound inextricably to the long struggle from slavery to integration.

There are other exceptional stories about black Americans in West Texas. Many of these stories, as in the case of Britt Johnson, are incomplete. While Johnson's life was portrayed in an article in *The New Handbook of Texas* and served as the basis for John Wayne's movie, *The Searchers*, Matt Braun's novel *Black Fox*, and a six-hour CBS mini-series, the stories of other black West Texans remain untold. Some unfortunately will remain unknown, but new evidence and new stories are forthcoming each year, including those by authors writing for the *West Texas Historical Association Year Book*.

Black Americans entered what is today West Texas as early as Estevan's incursion with Cabeza de Vaca in 1534-1536, and they accompanied other Spanish explorers into West Texas. Black soldiers with Francisco Vasquez de Coronado in 1540-1541 were the first to visit the region around Lubbock. During the mid-nineteenth century Southerners brought black slaves, such as Britt Johnson, to the region, and the numbers of black Americans in West Texas slowly expanded. Growth of the African-Texan population increased after the Civil War with the arrival of black cowboys, black soldiers, and black Seminole Indians. Some black families also settled in West Texas. In the early twentieth century opportunities with the railroads and in the oil fields offered avenues of employment. A few African Americans ranched, farmed, or settled in small communities. As the twentieth century progressed, blacks in West Texas moved to the region's cities; their work and their energy aided in the growth and prosperity of such communities as Abilene, Amarillo, El Paso, Lubbock, Midland, Odessa, San Angelo, and Wichita Falls.

Despite their numbers and their contributions, there is as yet no overall published history of black Americans in West Texas. That is not to say that books and monographs have not been produced on African Americans in the region. Although, with the exception of Britt Johnson, little is known about pre-Civil War black West Texans, works on the African American experience in post-Civil War Texas have nonetheless expanded our knowledge.[6]

Scholars who have studied the buffalo soldiers—the black troopers who helped to transform West Texas—especially add to our knowledge. Paul H. Carlson, in two studies, *"Pecos Bill": A Military Biography of William R. Shafter* (Texas A&M Press, 1989) and *The Buffalo Soldier Tragedy of 1877* (Texas A&M Press, 2003) depicts the life and work of these soldiers. Harold Ray Sayre, in *Warriors of Color* (privately printed, 1995), located much information about the buffalo soldiers during their stay at Fort Davis in the 1880s. Garna L. Christian covered the violent reaction created by white and brown opposition to the black soldiers in his work, *Black Soldiers in Jim Crow Texas, 1899-1917* (Texas A&M Press, 1995).

Recently, James N. Leiker pointed to the multiplicity of cultures and their interactions in *Racial Borders: Black Soldiers along the Rio Grande* (Texas A&M Press, 2002). He reminded us that West Texas, perhaps more than the remainder of the state, was a land where black, brown, red, and white interacted and confronted each other. The saga of black soldiers in West Texas can also be found in Thomas A. Britten's *A Brief History of the Seminole-Negro Indian Scouts* (Mellen Press, 1999), and additional information on the scouts and their families can be found in Jeff Guinn, *Our Land Before We Die: The Proud Story of the Seminole Negro* (J.P. Tarcher/Putnam, 2002).

Britt Johnson worked on a West Texas ranch as did other black Americans in the late nineteenth and early twentieth centuries. Both the black cowboys and ranchers have been portrayed in monographs. Hettye Wallace Branch, for instance, published a biography of her father, *The Story of "80 John": A Biography of One of the Most Respected Negro Ranchmen in the Old West* (Greenwich, 1960). Bruce G. Todd wrote *Bones Hooks: Pioneer Negro Cowboy* (Pelican, 2005). Hooks was one of the first blacks to work and live in Amarillo. Elmer Kelton explores the explosive relationship between a white and black cowboy on the West Texas plains in his riveting novel, *Wagontongue* (Bantam, 1972), and his majestic western *The Wolf and the Buffalo* (Doubleday, 1980) wrestles with the competing worlds of a black soldier and a Commanche warrior as their paths cross in the West.

Though black Americans worked on farms and ranches, on the railroads, and in the oil fields during the twentieth century, most of the existing studies of such West Texas experiences focus on African Americans in urban communities of the region. Two books on blacks in Abilene help to understand life in that city: Beatrice Walker, *Who's Who Among Blacks of Abilene* (Abilene Copy Shop, 1991), and Jewell G. Pritchett, *The Black Community of Abilene* (Pritchett, 1984). Black Wichita Falls also has been covered in C. Emerson Jackson and Gwendolyn M. Jackson, *The History of the Negro, Wichita Falls, Texas, 1880-1982* (Humphrey Printing, 1989, 2003). On black Lubbock, see Katie Parks, *Remember When? A History of African Americans in Lubbock, Texas* (Texas Tech Southwest Collection, 1999).

Perhaps due to its prominent location, a number of works from El Paso have emerged. An oral history of black El Paso women, edited by Maceo C. Dailey, Jr., and Kristine Navarro, *Wheresoever My People Chance to Dwell: Oral Interviews with African American Women of El Paso* (Black Classic, 2000), adds to our understanding of both black West Texas women and the border city. Another El Paso woman, Bernice Love Wiggins, wrote poetry. Her delightful book of poems, *Tuneful Tales*, was privately published in 1925. More recently, Maceo C. Dailey, Jr., and Ruthe Winegarten edited Wiggins' book and in 2002 Texas Tech University Press reprinted it in its Double Mountain Books series.

As was true of their experiences elsewhere in the state, black Americans in rural areas and in the cities and towns of West Texas lacked voting rights. El Paso blacks, with support from the National Association for the Advancement of Colored People (NAACP) especially were prominent in the fight against suffrage restriction. It is a topic covered in Conrey Bryson's informative *Dr. Lawrence A. Nixon and the White Primary* (Texas Western, 1974). West Texans led in integration activities as well, including that Texas passion, athletic contests. The Texas Western College saga of its basketball team's primarily black athletes, coached by Don Haskins, and its victory over a team of white Kentucky players for the 1966 NCAA basketball championship is portrayed in at least three books: Don Haskins and Dan Wetzel, *Glory Road* (Hyperion, 2006), Frank Fitzpatrick, *And the Walls Came Tumbling Down* (Nebraska, 1999), and in Ray Sanchez, *Basketball's Biggest Upset* (Mesa, 1991).

From Britt Johnson's travails through racial incidents against black soldiers to suffrage restrictions, black West Texans lived with racial prejudice and injustice. One black cowboy was lynched for marrying a white woman, Lt. Henry O. Flipper was unfairly discharged from the army, black Americans attended segregated schools, and employment opportunities for black West Texans were limited.

Unfortunately, in 2007 such racist behavior persists. In a series of highly corrupt and dishonorable arrests a dishonest investigator accused black Americans in Tulia of drug peddling and smuggling. Subsequently, the courts convicted the defendants and sentenced them to time in prison. When rumors of perverted justice came to light, the government sought to release the long-suffering prisoners and return them to their homes. Nate Blakesley in *Tulia: Race, Cocaine, and Corruption in a Small Texas Town* (Public Affairs Press, 2005) describes the sorry episode.

While scholars continue to contribute books and monographs on black West Texans, much of the scholarly research and writing on the subject is published in the region's academic journals. Such publications include, but are not limited to, the *Journal of Big Bend Studies*, the *Panhandle-Plains Historical Review*, *Password*, and the *West Texas Historical Association Year Book*, the oldest journal in the western part of the state. In fact, the annual *Year Book* contains the most extensive coverage of African American history for the region.

The West Texas Historical Association was headquartered for many years at Hardin-Simmons University in Abilene, but in 1997 the Association, under the leadership of B.W. Aston and Paul H.

Carlson, moved its offices to Texas Tech University. Founded in 1924, its early leaders included R.C. Crane, Rupert N. Richardson, Carl Coke Rister, William Curry Holden, Mrs. Dallas Scarborough, Fred Cockrell, John Hutto, Mrs. L.M. Stevenson, and L.B. Kennamer.

From its beginning, the Association has produced a journal. Volume one came out in 1925, and others have appeared annually since then. In the early years of the Association's *Year Book*, a publications committee selected the articles to include and assigned one of its members the responsibility of editing them for publication. Although the Association did not list an official editor until 1960, Richardson edited the first volume; Rister volumes two, three, and four; and Richardson thereafter until 1974 when B.W. Aston, chair of the Hardin-Simmons history department, became secretary-treasurer of the Association and editor of the *Year Book*. Kenneth Jacobs, Paul H. Carlson, and Monte L. Monroe, who became editor in 2003, followed Aston.

Meanwhile, working from his office at Hardin-Simmons University, Richardson, called the Dean of Texas Historians, almost single-handedly managed the editorial chores and in general ran the Association. If R.C. Crane, who served as president of the organization from 1925 to 1949, is credited with "fathering" the West Texas Historical Association, Richardson, as Ernest Wallace has written, "was the widowed 'Mother.'" In addition to his editorial duties, Rupert N. Richardson nurtured and guided the Association, "made most of the major decisions . . . regarding the programs," membership dues, and affairs of the annual conference.[7]

In terms of editorial content, Richardson and Aston and the other editors always sought articles on minority topics. As a result, beginning in the early 1930s pieces appeared in the *Year Book* covering black American topics. And during the 1960s, perhaps in response to the growing American civil rights movement, such pieces became more frequent. Currently, over thirty articles related to African American experiences in West Texas have been published in the *West Texas Historical Association Year Book*. The articles cover the main themes of West Texas and United States western history. They include such topics as slavery, black soldiers, black Seminole Indian scouts, black cowboys, integration into communities and schools, white racism, black protest and resistance, and rural to urban migration.

Noticeable in the studies, as well as the experiences, of blacks in West Texas are the variations from statewide (and even national) trends. Few slaves existed in West Texas. The post-Civil War economic livelihood of East Texas blacks—sharecropping—did not extend to West Texas. Black and white West Texans avoided much of the bitter black/white struggle that took place during Reconstruction. Lynchings and race riots and whitecappings, though occasional, did not dominate white/black behavior in the western part of the state. Perhaps the most important reasons for the differences related to the topology, the climate, and the environment. Neither blacks nor whites arrived in West Texas in large numbers, they did not focus their economy on cotton (until later in the twentieth century), and the concept of western openness and freedom aided black American achievement.

Twelve articles selected from the *West Texas Historical Association Year Book* form the basis for this book: *Slavery to Integration: Black Americans in West Texas*. In addition, there is a list of other scholarly essays about black Americans in West Texas appearing in the *Year Book*. The twelve selected articles, organized chronologically, track black West Texans from slavery to integration and cover major topics and themes associated with African Americans in the region.[8] Read individually, each explores an important aspect of African American history in West Texas and, read in aggregate, they cover black West Texas history broadly.

The first article explores slavery in West Texas. Before 1865, some of West Texas was unorganized, and there were few inhabitants in the unorganized parts. Even in Young County (Britt Johnson's home), as Barbara A. Ledbetter notes in "Black and Mexican Slaves in Young County, Texas, 1856-1865," the number of slaves was small, and some were Mexican, not African. Slavery did not constitute the economic framework for West Texas as it did for much of the remainder of the state, or the South. It was much more attuned to the entrepreneurial resource usage of other parts of the western United States. Even in El Paso County, the number of slaves in 1860 numbered only eight.

After the Civil War, one of the occupations that opened to African Americans in West Texas, as it did earlier for Britt Johnson, was that of cowboy and rancher. Two articles in this collection focus on their lives. The first, contributed by R.C. Crane, is a brief reminiscence from D.W. "80 John" Wallace, a black cowhand and rancher who eventually settled in Mitchell County. Entitled "D.W. Wallace ("80 John"): an African American Cattleman on the Texas Frontier," the memoir details life while working cattle on the ranges of West Texas. The next article, Lawrence Clayton's "Nig London: Throckmorton County Cowman," portrays the emergence of a successful black rancher in the West Texas county.

Soldiering was another late nineteenth century occupation open to blacks. Called Buffalo Soldiers, the black troopers contributed significantly to protecting West Texas inhabitants and to expanding the population westward. Yet too often they faced discrimination from those they were charged to protect. Paul H. Carlson, in "William R. Shafter Commanding Black Troops in West Texas," describes the relationship between Col. William R. Shafter and the black soldiers as well as the aggressiveness in how Shafter drove his troopers. But, the soldiers persevered and their efforts helped secure the Mexico-Texas border.

Almost all commissioned officers of the black units were white; one of the few exceptions was Lt. Henry O. Flipper, the first black graduate of West Point. Despite his exemplary career, white officers court-martialed and dishonorably discharged Flipper from the army for conduct unbecoming an officer. Ironically, his commander, usually known as a supporter of his black troops, was Colonel Shafter. Donald R. McClung covers Flipper's life and career in "Second Lieutenant Henry O. Flipper: A Black Officer on the West Texas Frontier."

Black soldiers commonly received tedious and sometimes dangerous duties, but in their posts they could relax, and as time permitted, engage in recreational activities. But, their very presence often infuriated whites concerned at the prospect of armed blacks in their midst. Racial incidents sometimes occurred. In "Blacks in San Angelo: Relations between Fort Concho and the City, 1875-1889," Patricia E. Gower examines the flammable relations that existed between black soldiers and white community members.

In 1870 other black soldiers joined the ranks of the United States Army when black Seminoles, then residing in Mexico, returned to the United States. In a treaty, perhaps, the black Seminoles agreed to work as scouts for the U.S. Army. In return, the United States would provide their families with food, basic necessities for living, and ultimately land. In a pattern repeated in U.S.-Indian relations in the West, the agreement was not honored. Eric Emmerson Strong in "The Lost Treaty of the Black Seminoles" points out that govenment officials never provided the land, and the treaty apparently disappeared, or, as some whites contended, never existed.

Black cowboys, buffalo soldiers, and black Seminole scouts typified black American individuals who lived and worked in West Texas during the latter nineteenth century. In the twentieth century, more and more African Americans moved into cities of the region. The influx, in turn, gave rise to additional difficulties, including inaccurate population counts. In Abilene in 1900, the United States Census takers undercounted both white and black residents. Karen Turner in "Abilene's Minority Population and the 1900 Census" explains the inaccuracies and in the process provides a case study of the black population of Abilene during the first decade of the twentieth century.

The growing black American population of West Texas cities in the twentieth century is a rich field for scholarly investigation. Robert L. Foster and Alwyn Barr describe the twentieth century growth of the black population of Lubbock in their simply titled article, "Black Lubbock." Although the facts and data described are for Lubbock, many of the experiences in general fit the patterns in the black communities of other West Texas cities, such as Abilene, Amarillo, and Wichita Falls.

Education was an important aspect of African American needs in any community and especially in West Texas where segregated schools were mandated by state law. June M. Steele concentrated on two black leaders and their efforts to ensure the success of black educational opportunities in Lubbock in her excellent article, "Edward Struggs and Mae Simmons: Two African American Educators and the Provisions for Black Schools in Lubbock, Texas, 1930-1970."

A long range goal for black educators and leaders in West Texas, as elsewhere in the country, was integration of the schools. Area communities responded differently to this black aspiration and to the 1954 *Brown v. Board of Education* decision that determined separate schools were unconstitutional. In one community, San Angelo, as Gregory A. Doherty in "The Beginnings of Integration in San Angelo I.S.D." reports, white leaders facilitated the process without a struggle. In another, Odessa, whites resisted. The Odessa struggle for and against integrated schools is discussed in Bryan L. Smith, "Desegregation in West Texas: *The United States v. Ector County I.S.D. Case.*

While West Texas with its open range and late settlement offered opportunities to black Texans not available in the South generally, the black experience began with slavery and was fraught with economic uncertainty, state sanctioned inequitable treatment, and a mindset that condoned and accepted discriminatory treatment of its black citizens. By the latter years of the twentieth century, as integration efforts and decisions in San Angelo and Odessa indicate, black Americans in West Texas moved toward full integration within the larger white community. Such experiences provide a rich field for scholarly research and the *West Texas Historical Association Year Book* offers a publishing outlet. Such experiences also suggest that Britt Johnson's short and courageous life was not in vain.

NOTES

[1] Kenneth Neighbors, "Elm Creek Raid in Young County," *West Texas Historical Association Year Book* 40 (1964): 83-89.

[2] E. McClellan, "Britton Johnson," in *The New Handbook of Texas*, edited by Ron Tyler, et al (Austin: Texas State Historical Association, 1996), 2:160.

[3] Ibid., 3:952; Neighbors, "Elm Creek Raid in Young County," 88-89.

[4] Neighbors, "Elm Creek Raid in Young County," 88-89.

[5] Matt Braun, *Black Fox* (1972; New York: St. Martin's Paperbacks, 1994), ii.

[6] For a listing of works on blacks in West Texas, see Bruce A. Glasrud, "African-Americans in West Texas: A Selected Bibliography," *Journal of Big Bend Studies* 18 (2006): 191-212.

[7] Ernest Wallace, "The West Texas Historical Association," *West Texas Historical Association Year Book* 59 (1983): 10. See also Rupert N. Richardson, "Our First Fifty Years," *West Texas Historical Association Year Book* 50 (1974): 3-20.

[8] The authors of a number of these articles, including two of the editors, are products of the Texas Tech School of Black History. For more on this educational endeavor, see Bruce A. Glasrud and James M. Smallwood, "The Texas Tech School of Black History: An Overview," *West Texas Historical Association Year Book* 82 (2006): 102-19.

Black and Mexican Slaves in Young County, Texas, 1856-1865

Barbara A. Ledbetter

It has been said that Young County was not a slave-holding county, and hence its history has not been appreciably affected by slavery. However, if we consider its sparse population and its time of formation, we can see that it was indeed a rather large slave holding area. From 1856-1865, there was one black to every three white adults in the county.

In 1860, Young County's population was 624. This figure did not include blacks, military personnel, or rangers. Of this number, 298 were aged eighteen or over, and 172 were children who had been born in Texas.

Blacks came to Young County as a part of family wagon-trains. They worked as wagoners, cooks, teamsters, farm and ranch hands, wranglers, domestics, and woodcutters. One of their major contributions was to supply the labor force on the first roads cut across the county in all directions. Most African

Americans in this area were valued at 800 dollars each by their owners, but one old Tennessee widower, Moses Johnson, valued his black family (Britt Johnson's) of four at 2200 dollars. Whites owned thirty-two cabins or slave quarters in the county. For example, Mrs. Susan (Vannoy) Parks, a 70-year old widow, owned three cabins for her slaves on acreage along the Brazos.

The blacks in Young County were from one to four generations removed from their African ancestry, and they did not use surnames except for those they adopted from their patrons or masters. Although it was not a socially accepted practice, miscegenation was a sociological fact. It is an historical fact that one-fourth of the slaves in Young County were mulattoes.

Minorities in all parts of our nation have become interested in searching for their roots. Young County is no exception. Because of the lack of surnames and the changing of surnames among African Americans, it is very difficult for them to search for their ancestors. Therefore, it seems appropriate to compile information that might be beneficial for genealogical research.

Blacks, mulattoes, and Mexicans comprised most of the slaves in Young County. Blacks and mulattoes were owned by and/or took surnames of the following:

Allen	Fain	Marlin
Alverson	George	Matthews
Anderson	Gibbins	Miller
Bell	Gooch	Morris
Bly	Goodlet	Murphy
Bottorff	Hamner	Nance
Bowers	Harmonson	Oberchain
Bragg	Johnson	Parks
Carter	Kennedy	Peveler
Cochran	Latimer	Standefer
Crawford	Ledbetter	Thomas
Cureton	Luckey	Vollentine
Deckman	McKay	Williams
Duff	Manly	Young

The first names of all African Americans in Young County will never be known, but over a period of twenty-five years the author has found in widely scattered records the following:

Alex	Eliza	Maryann
Amanda	Ellen	Melinda
America	Ely	Milla
Anarcha	Floyd	Paint
Ann	Frank	Prince
Big Sam	Harriet	Rachel
Bill	Jefferson	Reuben
Britt	Jim	Richard
Charley	Lizzie	Rufus
Cherry	Lottie	Seth
Dennis	Louisia	Sol
Edmund	Lucy	Texana
Elija	Mary	

The author has found twelve first names for the seventeen Mexican slaves in Young County at this time. They are:

Bady	Dewarsey	Labrain
Berry	Guadulupe	Roffell
Dafratra	Ignatia	Virginia
Debotour	John	William

The 1858 records of the Young County District Court shed light on one of the most unusual cases in the state concerning African Americans. The case was "Ex Parte Rachel and Anarcha, free persons of color." It was a petition to the court to set aside a black husband's and black wife's status as "free persons of color," and in turn to make them "slaves forever." They wished to surrender their freedom and to become enslaved to one whom they considered to be kind, indulgent, supportive, their master, Commander 2nd Cavalry at Fort Belknap, Maj. George H. Thomas.

District Judge Nathaniel M. Burford weighed all evidence presented and concluded that Major Thomas would be a suitable master. He decreed that the blacks "should become the property of Major Thomas and his heirs and assigns forever." Since they had denounced and surrendered their sacred right to freedom, it can be concluded that when Major Thomas left Fort Belknap in February of 1859, first for Camp Cooper, thence to his home in the South and his rewards from the Civil War, he took his slaves Anarcha and Rachel with him.

After the Civil War, Young County was populated by a handful of Union veterans and many, many Confederate veterans. Slavery became a debatable subject instead of a viable practice in the county.

D.W. Wallace ("80 John")
An African American Cattleman on the Texas Frontier

Contributed by R.C. Crane

The following letter from Judge Crane serves as an introduction to this interesting item:

I enclose the sketch of the West Texas Outstanding African American, "80 John." My recollection is that our good friend Mrs. Lee Jones[1] got this for us back in 1934, and that D.W. Wallace, or "80 John" as he was known, died soon afterwards, owning at the time a ranch of some ten or twelve sections in south Mitchell County, two sections near Loraine, and half a dozen or so good farms and about 500 high grade Hereford cattle.

The sketch mentions Clay Mann (his boss) having a ranch on Silver Creek, a stream that rises in southwest Nolan County, runs southwestward through east Mitchell County into the Colorado River.

As I recall this sketch was actually written on "80 John's" dictation by a school teacher's daughter.

                        Yours, Sincerely,
                        R.C. CRANE.

I have been asked by several of my white friends to write the history of my life and the pioneer days in the west. I have been trying for ten years to decide on making the attempt to comply to their request. I have never been ashamed of my life, but I have always felt I could not tell the facts of the old pioneer days in an interesting way, even though I have grown up with the west.

I was born in Victoria County, Sept. 15, 1860, near Inez, Texas, on a small farm owned by a Mrs. Mary Cross. The farm consisted of about 200 acres, a few cows, and other stock. The houses on the farm were built of logs. The place where I stayed was a log house of two rooms and a small hall. All the rooms had dirt for floors. My parents worked on this farm.

When I was six years old, we moved with these people to a small town in Fayette County, near the present town of Flotonia.

While yet small I worked for a number of people with no pay as reward, as most of the people then did not believe in paying children for their labor.

In 1876 on the 13th day of March, I started to work for a Mr. Carr, who moved his family and a small herd of cattle to Lampasas County. After the work was over I left Mr. Carr with $1.50 in my pockets for Taylor County on the head of Jim Ned, where Tom Cross, the son of the woman on whose place I was born, was working for Sam Gholson. I stayed there and worked a year.

In July, a year later a Mr. John Nunn came by from South Texas hunting a place to stop. When he got in the neighborhood of Jim Ned the cattlemen there objected to his stopping and advised him to push on. He had about three boys who wanted to quit and go home. Their horses were poor and backs sore from the steady drives in the saddle. Nunn was a stranger in the country and didn't know much about frontier life. Gholson told him if he would move on a little further he would find plenty of country that no one claimed. Nunn spoke of his horses being in such a bad shape and some of his men wanting to quit, then, Gohlson told him he had a boy who could help him, as he didn't have much for him to do. On the 12th of July I went to work for the Nunn outfit. We moved about 18 miles from Jim Ned close to Mountain Pass, which is Southwest of Merkel. Staying there a few days we found that country stocked with other cattlemen, such as C.E. Oldham, Bill Isaac, Alec Martin, The Half Diamond H. Ranch on Elm Creek. They, too, objected to Nunn staying there, but in the meanwhile his cattle had gotten badly scattered. During the last week in September we got what cattle we could find and pulled out.

On the last day of September we stopped at Sand Rock Springs in Scurry County, ten or twelve miles east of the present town of Snyder. I worked for Nunn 17 months.

On the 12th of December 1878 I hired to a Mr. Clay Mann[2] who lived in Coleman County. The next spring he bought beef cattle and drove them to Whitesboro. Later he established a ranch near Silver Creek, a few miles south of Colorado City.

The Indians stole all of our horses in 1878 and most of them in 1879, but we stayed there all the year of 1880. On the 19th of January in 1881 Mann sold the J.D. Brand to a man by the name of J.W. Wilson. Mr. Mann then began to buy cattle and started the 80 brand. From this brand my friends gave me the name 80 John. The 80 brand ran to a large number, at one time Mr. Mann claimed to have 26,000 head of cattle. In 1883 he drove on the trail 4,000 cattle and established a ranch in Wyoming. In the spring of 1884 he drove about 4,000 more. These cattle were sold at Dodge, Kansas. Later he returned and drove in the fall about 1,000 head to Coffeyville, Kansas.

Life on the range was altogether different from what the people find today. Our homes were dugouts when we were fortunate to find one where a buffalo hunter had lived. Some times we would take time and build one, but more often we used our wagons and the ground. It was common to lie on the ground in all kinds of weather with our blankets for a bed and a saddle for a pillow.

There were no stores closer than 90 and 150 miles from our camps. Often times the boy's clothes would become worn before a chance to go or send to town. We would take sacks, rip them up and make pants. Some one usually went to Coleman City about every two or three months for food, clothes and other things we needed.

I have seen people on the frontier who had a narrow escape for their lives, yet they would stay. Everyone slept with his gun under his head. When a fellow grew tired of his gun or careless about where his cartridges were, he was turned off. An outfit would furnish you with a gun and cartridges, usually a pistol and Winchester; you were not allowed to shoot a rabbit or small game. Sometimes we had a nervous fellow in the bunch who would reach for his gun excitingly when a fellow would come to wake him up—after having stood guard for several hours.

Rattlesnakes and dangerous beasts were plentiful. It was common to find a snake rolled up in your bedding or be awakened early in the morning by the howl of the wolf or holler of the panther. Sometimes for fun the boys would rope a wolf.

I have stood guard dark, stormy nights when you couldn't see what you were guarding until a flash of lightning. Many times the cattle would stampede and in the rush, often the cattle or a cowboy was hurt.

Frequently the cattle could be gathered the next day, but I have seen it take two or three days to gather them. A man was considered lucky who got all of his bunch together. Sometimes herds would run together. I have seen eight or ten thousand head of cattle in one bunch.

When a sale was made on the range, the buyer brought his money in bags and counted it out. No checks were ever written. I have seen Mr. Mann with $10,000 in camp. I saw a man sell his cattle for eighty thousand dollars ($80,000). The buyer wanted to give the man an order for the money, but the owner of the cattle refused to take it saying, "If you want my cattle bring me the money." The buyer went after his money, came back with the cash. The cowman placed a blanket on the ground, the buyer counted out $80,000. The proud owner loaded everything he could take, hitched his oxen to a wagon and started to Brownwood with his money.

When an outfit paid the cowboys, some of them would go to town, drink, play games, later go to sleep, wake up the next morning hungry and broke, probably borrow a little change to eat before going back to work.

If a fellow got sick on the range, he just laid around camp until he got well or died. There were no doctors in the country. I have seen a pitiful sight of a cowboy groaning with pain while we stood around helpless, had nothing or knew nothing to lessen his misery.

In 1885 Mann thought he would establish a ranch in Old Mexico. He went out early in the winter to locate the place in company with G.K. Elkins, his father-in-law; Willis Halliway; Hiram Adams; and John Good. No one bought a ranch except Mr. Mann and Elkins. In the spring they started to stock that ranch and placed about 4,000 cattle there, landing with the cattle the 25th of August.

We had a hard trip driving across the desert country. We drove 90 miles without a drop of water. When we got a way over in Mexico we began to meet a large number of Mexicans. They didn't understand where we were going. We tried to explain to them that we were going to Barvequero Lake. When they understood they told us that we couldn't live there, that there were plenty of Indians who had killed all the people who tried to live there. We knew not what to do, but go on where Mann told us to go, with Rainey, the man in charge. We traveled on, arriving on the 25th of August. We built a house of pine logs, covered with dirt. For days we hadn't seen any Indians, but every night we watched for them, sleeping by turns. We felt that the Indian scare was a method the Mexicans used to run us out of the country. But on the 18th day of October, the Indians appeared, raided our camp, burned our wagons and pens, killed our milk cows, took all the horses we weren't riding and waylaid us in the hills. The Indians hid themselves under a large rock, as we began to pass by means of a narrow trail. John Mann, was the first man who passed, riding a little pony of mine. The Indians killed Mann and the next fellow to follow in the trail, John Clairon and both horses. The rest of us ran as fast as we could to the prairie, away from the mountains. We felt safer in the open as Indians always hid themselves to make an attack. As quickly as we could we buried the boys in shallow graves. Later we picked up their bones where wolves had dug them out, placed them in a box and buried them again.

One day while riding in a deep canyon we saw signs of horses. The horses were wild as bucks, closely looking we saw they were branded. The horses belonged to the Eighties. Out of three, one was mine. Later some men who crossed the high mountains from the state of Sonora into Chihuahua found some horses with the 80 brand that had been stolen from the Mann ranch by Indians.

We saw some interesting places in Mexico. One day while riding we were told by some prospectors searching for gold of a canyon where people had once inhabited. This place was about 20 or 30 feet deep. We visited this canyon by letting one another down and up by drawing ropes. You could tell that people had lived there, but it looked like hundreds of years ago.

Mann kept the ranch in Mexico until 1886 and sold it to a Mr. Hearst who is the present owner. Most of us came back to Texas and were glad to get back. Mann held his ranches in Mitchell and Kent Counties, moving large herds of cattle to New Mexico.

In 1889, sometime in July Mr. Mann died. I worked for the Mann outfit 22 years.

In 1888 I married Laura D. Owens near Hubbard City, in Hill County. We have four children and four grandchildren.

I went to school very little, when I was young. Schools were scarce. I received most of my learning by contact with others and observation. I have a method of figuring of my own which has held me in good stead; very seldom I have missed anything due me any larger than a fraction.

I have grown up with the horse and the cow. I still like outdoor life. Very seldom a day passes that I don't mount my horse and ride for hours.

      D.W. Wallace
      Mitchell County, Loraine, Texas.

NOTES

[1] See the *West Texas Historical Association Year Book* for 1943, pp. 86ff.
[2] See the *West Texas Historical Association Year Book* for 1948, p. 88.

Nig London: Throckmorton County Cowman

Lawrence Clayton

Anyone who thinks that all the old-time cowmen are gone has not met Nig London of Throckmorton. Mr. London has been a cowboy and cowman all his life and, he says, if he had it to do again, he would do it just the same way. He has operated a ranch of his own along with overseeing large leased ranches and herds of cattle, particularly steers, with a partner. At eighty years of age he still sees after his own cattle, rides his horses, and watches over a fine stretch of cattle country in Throckmorton County of West Texas, where he was born on a small family ranch along Hog Creek in 1910.

Mr. London can remember much about his days on the range. His most memorable experience involved a drive of 1800 steers from the Nail Ranch, just north of Albany in Shackelford County, back to Throckmorton County range in 1923. He was only thirteen years old at the time, but he remembers that his father gathered the saddle horses and a chuck wagon and made the two-day trip to the area along the Clear Fork of the Brazos. The outfit spent the first night near the site of old Camp Cooper, just north of the Matthews' Lambshead Ranch. George Wright had the land leased at the time. The next morning they crossed the river and rode on to the Nail Ranch to the south. Francis Gober, who had worked for Judge J.A. Matthews for thirty-five years, led the party through the area because he knew all the crossings, gates, and natural barriers. As they crossed the river bottom, the horse herd went through heavy stands of cockleburrs. That night as Mr. Nail looked at the night horses in the corral, he inquired about the cockleburrs. He then told Mr. London's father to wrangle the entire remuda and get all the cockleburrs out of their tails. Mr. London remembers that it took way up into the night to remove all the cockleburrs, which were then burned. Mr. Nail had fought the pesky plants for years and did not want new seed brought to his range.

The steers were gathered out of a large pasture, and Talmadge Palmer, mounted a fine sorrel horse, cut out the 1800 head. These were cut out individually, and when a group of 400 was cut out, it was driven some distance to the north away from the herd so that the danger of becoming mixed with the larger group was not possible. Mr. London remembers that the fine cutting horse had a technique that when each animal was cut out, the horse bowed his head to that animal before being reined back into the herd to select another.

As is characteristic of all cowboys, Mr. London has been interested in horses all of his life. When he was barely thirteen years old, he and his younger brother broke nine head of horses for the neighboring Davis ranch. The techniques employed by the boys, though differing noticeably from the more recently developed Ray Hunt technique, were nonetheless effective and widely used. Late in the afternoon the boys would rope one horse and snub it down to a post. Then they would put a hackamore on the animal. This rope hackamore, which Mr. London's father made by hand, was constructed of "nickel ropel," a small grass rope, and included a nose band and brow band, and was securely attached to the animal's head. A lead rope some twenty feet long was then attached to a rock large enough that the horse could drag it with considerable effort, but not so large that the animal would risk a broken neck by tugging against it during the night. By the next morning the animal's nose would be sore from pulling against the weight and his attention more easily gained by the lads. The youngsters would then take the horse to a round pen for the next step. To saddle the animal, the boys snubbed it to a post and tied a rope around the horse's neck and then got a rope around one of the horse's rear feet. By running that second piece of rope through the loop around the horse's neck, they could draw one hind foot off the ground, thereby incapacitating the animal for saddling. Once the saddle was in place, a task which might take considerable time, one of the boys would mount the horse and ride it. If pitched off, they had no choice but to get back on. They would ride the horse in a small pen and then a larger pen, and, depending on the temperament of the individual animal, would eventually turn it out and ride it in the trap and later the big pasture. Through this process Mr. London and his younger brother spent an entire summer breaking and gentling nine horses. For this job, they were paid the sum of $5.00 per horse.

He remembers when conscious efforts were made to upgrade the quality of horses available in the Throckmorton area. Mr. Davis, an area rancher, bought a high quality Yellow Wolf stallion from the Waggoner Ranch at Vernon to breed to his mares, many of which were of Spanish stock or mustangs. There was also a government breeding station at Seymour that kept two jacks, two Percheron, and two thoroughbred stallions. These sires were available to area farmers and ranchers and represented an effort by the government to upgrade the bloodlines of horses available to people in a time when quality horseflesh was not a luxury but a necessity. The larger horses that resulted from this breeding program became work animals, and the smaller ones became saddle horses. Part of the motivation of the government was to secure remounts for the U.S. cavalry.

Mr. London recounts seeing numerous paint horses when he was younger and then saw most of them disappear as selective breeding tended to favor solid colors—bays, sorrels, blacks, and browns. Now that cycle seems to be coming full circle because most ranch herds contain at least one paint horse.

Cowboy gear and equipment has not altered much in Mr. London's recollection. He can recall a good many saddles, old when he was a boy, that were slick-forked or A-fork saddles. He responded to my question about bucking rolls that he did not see them used on the old saddles, but many people tied a coat across the front of the saddle to pad them against the horn and to act as a barrier to being pitched off over the front of the saddle. Most of the saddles that he has seen all of his life had at least some swell in fork and typically a rolled cantle. Two of the favorite makers were Turnsal of Miles City, Montana, and R.T. Frazier of Pueblo, Colorado.

The spurs he has been familiar with most of his life sported short shanks and small rowels. The chaps, in early days, were batwings, but he later saw a transition to the shotgun style. He said initially the shotguns were just sewn down the side and were not preferred by cowboys because whatever was on the cowboy's boots was smeared inside the leg as the foot passed through. It wasn't until full-length zippers were added to the shotguns that cowboys definitely came to prefer them over the batwings. Mr. London has seen the shorter chink chaps come in but has not seen them gain the popularity still retained by the shotgun style. In traditional cowboy fashion, he wore boots made by Bud Humphries, a long-time maker at Seymour.

Of other cowboy gear, Mr. London has strong recollections. He remembers that when he started out, most cowboys had only one bridle and used it on all their mounts. He said these days it sometimes takes a pickup to haul all the cowboys' bridles, since they still have several styles of headstall as well as several different kinds of bits.

I asked Mr. London specifically about the length of lariat ropes. He said that ranches kept a coil of rope, and when a cowboy needed a new lariat, the boss simply cut off 33 feet of rope. The typical pattern of roping cattle was to tie hard and fast, in the Texas fashion, and not to dally, a technique that has come to this region more recently, particularly with team ropers in arena settings. Some cowboys have adopted the technique for pasture work as well.

The working methods for cattle when branding have not changed that much. Mr. London can remember the first working chute that was brought into the region by R.A. Brown for his large ranch in southern Throckmorton County around 1915. But Mr. London's early experience usually involved roping and dragging. The small calves were neck-roped; the larger calves were heeled. It was not uncommon to get smaller calves into a crowing pen and simply neck them down and work them, a technique still used by some today, and not unknown in some areas of northeastern Mexico, as recounted by one of my informants.

Mr. London agrees that World War II wrought the greatest change to life of the cowboy. It was at this time that horse trailers became widely used for hauling horses from one ranch to another. Only later did the practice develop of hauling horses from the headquarters to the pasture to be worked. Cattle came to be more frequently hauled rather than driven, even for short distances on the ranch during workings. Mr. London credits some of the change to welding techniques learned by men in the service and taught to veterans under provisions of the G.I. Bill. The effect is particularly apparent in areas where oil production has been prominent because of the availability of pipe and other materials for fabrication using welding techniques. Other forms of mechanization became common, and most allowed less manpower to run the ranching operation. The drives to the railroad corrals were also eliminated by the use of truck and large trailers. Several factors were at work in this change. Mr. London has seen watering facilities go from shallow tanks scooped out by teams of mules pulling fresnos, to deeper, more efficient tanks dug by bulldozers.

The most significant alteration to cowboy life has been the eradication of screw worms. Mr. London remembers how ranchers changed their breeding cycle so that calves would be born during the cold months when worms were not a threat. But he also recalls how much gentler cattle became once cowboys could quit prowling pastures and roping calves to doctor screw worms. No one misses the ubiquitous bottle of Smear 62 or other such medicine tied to a saddle in a boot top cut off and laced up across the bottom.

The marketing of cattle has also undergone significant change. Mr. London remembers when all cattle were shipped to the Fort Worth yard. Later, regional auction rings opened. The first he recalls was in 1936 at Vernon. He said at first the auctions operated what he calls a "skin game" in which the sellers were manipulated by organized buyers. Later, however, as other auction rings opened in Wichita Falls, Munday, and Olney, the competition forced honesty on the part of the auction ring in order to attract buyers, and the shysters were soon driven out of business. Now ranchers can ship small numbers of calves to local markets, though they may choose to sell large lots of calves or steers to buyers for feed lots.

Mr. London is a perceptive cowboy, ranchman, and entrepreneur. He showed his good business sense in stating the qualities of a good cowboy. He said that some, of course, are better than others. He remembers that the only time he got into trouble was asking a man to do something that man couldn't do, or asking a man to do more than that man could do. That's a lesson some managers these days might take a lesson from, one of many we might learn from studying the life of old-time ranchers and cowboys who not only persisted but thrived during hard times and good to take their place with the living legends of the American West.

William R. Shafter Commanding Black Troops in West Texas

Paul H. Carlson

From the West Texas Plains in the mid-1870's Capt. Theodore Baldwin complained to his wife, "I do not think you would like to scout with Colonel Shafter."[1] The note was understated indeed. A martinet of force and persistence, Lt. Col. William R. Shafter of the Twenty-fourth United States Infantry Regiment always drove vigorously the black troops of his command. Many young officers, such as Captain Baldwin, grumbled about his dogged determination.

Typical of Shafter's drive was an episode in 1875. Upon leaving Casas Amarillas Lake, near present Littlefield on the Llano Estacado, in a southwesterly direction, Shafter had hoped to find sufficient water for his men and horses in the large circular depressions characteristic of the High Plains. During the first two days he was successful, but having found no water by the expiration of the third day, he concluded that he must either strike for the Pecos or turn back. Characteristically, the resolute officer ordered his black command to make for the Pecos some eighty miles distant. During the following two days and one night of marching, the troops suffered desperately from heat, dust, and thirst. On the last night out, many of the officers, having lost all hope of reaching the river, wrote messages to be taken home by those fortunate enough to survive.[2] Worn men were tied in their saddles; others at gun point were forced to keep up. Shafter cajoled, wheedled, and drove his men. After great hardship and privation, everyone safely, but exhaustively, reached the river.[3] In such aggressive style for more than a decade Shafter directed African American troops.

His black infantry in West Texas, however, was not the first that Shafter had led. During the Civil War he had enjoyed command of a volunteer unit and afterwards in Louisiana with the colorful Ranald Mackenzie had organized and trained one of the regular army's first all black regiments.[4] In 1867 with his troops he had been ordered to the lower Rio Grande and the following year moved to West Texas at Fort Clark.

As a subaltern to Ranald Mackenzie, Shafter at first had few field assignments. But with each opportunity to command he relentlessly pursued horse thieves, cattle rustlers, desperadoes, or Indian raiders who were ravaging the West Texas frontier. As one result he quickly became recognized as the most energetic man of his rank in the Department of Texas. As another he was soon considered a rough, insensitive commander of black troops who, to achieve a sense of discipline, did not hesitate to exert extraordinary and ruthless power.[5] In 1870 his reputation followed him to Fort Concho, at present San Angelo.

Here, the post surgeon was amazed at the energy and restlessness with which Shafter attacked his garrison chores. In his report for January 1870, the surgeon wrote that Shafter "has displayed an abundance of energy, devoting the first days of arrival to thoroughly policing the post . . . [and] seeing a large corral . . .

in the process of construction. . . . "⁶ In the weeks that followed Shafter continued to push his black command in construction activities. The next month, the surgeon reported that "work upon the guard house and corral is progressing with unprecedented rapidity. . . ."⁷

Vigorous and efficient in his post command, Shafter likewise was energetic in the field. In mid-August, after being ordered to Fort McKavett, he planned to scour thoroughly the lower Pecos River. Taking six officers and 128 enlisted men of the Ninth Cavalry and Twenty-fourth Infantry, he marched southwestward to the river, reaching it at a point about twenty miles below present Sheffield.

Here, Shafter temporarily divided his command. Leaving most of it in camp at the Pecos, he and Capt. Edward M. Heyl, Ninth Cavalry, with fifteen men crossed to the west bank of the river, climbed up onto the table lands, and marched due south for twenty miles, keeping all the time within four miles of the river. Using his field glasses to examine each ravine, Shafter discovered no indications of Indians. There, he left the river and rode southwestward for six or seven miles to Painted Rock Arroyo, only ten miles from the Rio Grande. Again finding no signs of Indians, with his patrol he returned to the rendezvous camp.

For nearly a month afterwards the command scouted in the vicinity of the lower Pecos. The hard-driving Shafter ordered his men to check every ravine. It was monotonous, exhausting work. No Indians were seen, neither were there trails nor other indications of Indians having passed through the country recently. Nevertheless, Shafter doggedly pushed his men to the task. The persistence brought some luck: eight Indian ponies, which Shafter estimated had been near the Pecos for six months, were caught.

In mid-September, unable to locate either Indians or recent signs of them, Shafter finally directed his tired troops back toward Fort McKavett. While returning, his scouts located several abandoned Indian villages, about thirty-five miles west of the headwaters of the North and South Llano rivers. One had contained possibly as many as 150 Indians. Nearby they discovered a large, permanent body of water about two hundred yards long and deep enough to swim horses. For years the army had heard reports of the water pond, but its location had been known only to the red men. Consequently the pond was a favorite and secure place for Indians who committed depredations in the country near the headwaters of the Nueces.[8]

The Pecos River campaign proved significant. Having marched nearly five hundred miles, the scout showed that no Indians were lurking in the vicinity of the Pecos and the headwaters of the Llano rivers. Eight horses had been captured. A strategic and favorite Indian camping place had been located, and no longer would the Indians be able to use the water hole as a safe rendezvous. Moreover, in the psychological warfare that figured vitally in Indian fighting, the expedition demonstrated to the Plains warriors that bluecoat troopers could campaign successfully in an area that Indians previously had thought inaccessible to the army.

Twice the following year Shafter led black soldiers into such supposedly impenetrable lands. In June 1871 with a command totaling eighty-six officers and enlisted men, he turned a routine pursuit of Comanche horse thieves into a major exploration of the Monahans Sand Hills and across the Llano Estacado.[9] He destroyed an abandoned Indian village, two dozen buffalo robes, skins, and a large supply of provisions. He captured twenty horses and mules. He discovered that Comanches and Lipan and Mescalero Apaches, longtime enemies, had concluded a peace in the Sand Hills and that *Comancheros* used the area as a place of barter.[10]

A month later Shafter penetrated another Indian sanctuary. This time he drove his black command from Fort Davis on an exhausting five hundred mile scout into the torrid Big Bend region of the Rio Grande. Here with his troops he explored the country, crossing and recrossing trails, noting important water holes, and marking the sites of old Indian camps. At San Vincente he discovered an important Apache crossing on the river. He reported abandoned Indian encampments twenty-five miles southwest of Pena Blanca. The grass along his line of march was excellent, but the only wood he found was very large cottonwood trees along the streams. Where he struck the Rio Grande, there was no timber.[11]

Although it had killed no Indians, the expedition had found abundant evidence that Apaches used the Big Bend as a sanctuary. Perhaps more important, Shafter added considerably to the geographical knowledge of the *Chihuahuan* deserts and Big Bend mountains. Indeed, the information he gained about their nature and resources enabled the army later to maneuver more confidently in the region. In addition, it smoothed the way for later settlement.[12]

No sooner had Shafter returned to Fort Davis than an Apache chief, who frequented the Big Bend and who had gone to Presidio to negotiate with the Mexican authorities for release of some children captives of his band, sent word from Presidio del Norte that he wished to surrender. Shafter sent Lt. Isaiah H. McDonald to receive the surrender. But perhaps because the Mexican residents there, who gained their living largely by supplying United States Army posts, did not welcome complete harmony between Indians and Americans, the *alcalde* of Presidio warned the chief that his departure would prejudice release of the children. Whatever the reason, McDonald returned to Fort Davis empty-handed. Shafter agreed with his lieutenant that "the local authorities at Del Norte do not want [the Apache] to make or keep peace with the United States."[13]

Meanwhile, at Fort Davis Shafter was active. He supervised the repair of buildings, the construction of corrals, and the remodeling of the hospital. In addition, whenever necessary, he protected his black Negro troops against racial injustice and discrimination. In one incident he took the stage coach lines to task. The infantry in the West was often assigned to guard stage lines. At the end of such a tour of duty men usually returned to the post on an inbound stage. Unfortunately, Shafter's black troops at least once were kept off the stage and forced to walk back to the barracks. Indeed, the El Paso Mail Lines station keeper at Leon Hole refused to provide food and shelter for the station guards. The tempestuous Shafter became incensed and immediately warned the stage company officers against further discrimination toward his men. When the black guards were put off the stage, he wrote, they were obliged to walk to Fort Stockton and along the way to obtain their rations "by their wits." He demanded that his troops should "be fed by the company or allowed facilities at the stations for cooking their own rations. . . ."[14] He would "be glad to furnish mail escorts as long as they are wanted," he concluded, "but they must be properly treated."[15] Apparently his letter got results for the records show no further complaint against the stage company.

In another incident Shafter challenged civilian authorities. When the volatile sheriff of Presidio County injudiciously entered Fort Davis to arrest a black soldier for public drunkenness, Shafter, aware that the bluecoat would be summarily prosecuted, would not allow the officer to remove the trooper. Although such belligerency represented a serious breach of military discipline, Shafter refused to subject his troops to what he regarded as legal hazing.[16]

The consequences proved critical. Although the trooper was never arrested, Shafter was immediately removed from Fort Davis. Later, the incident may have been included as evidence to deny him an early graduation to the rank of colonel. Much later, in 1887, after he had obtained the colonelcy, the incident apparently was offered as one excuse to block his promotion to the rank of brigadier general.[17]

Although temporarily rebuked, Shafter was not forgotten. Since the Department of Texas needed durable, effective officers, in the summer and fall of 1872 with his crack command of black troops he teamed for three months with Ranald Mackenzie on the Llano Estacado. While Mackenzie with one force scouted the Palo Duro and crossed the High Plains to Fort Sumner and beyond, Shafter with another examined the Caprock escarpment along the Salt Fork (Main Fork) of the Brazos. His black command made certain that there were no Indians lurking at the foot of the Staked Plains, although it found abundant evidence of old Indian camps near all the springs it visited. In addition, the command located water and fuel supplies and for future operations in the vicinity of present day Slaton and Lubbock made a map of the country scouted.[18]

The following year Shafter with his black troops aided Mackenzie again. This time he helped during preparations for the celebrated raid into Mexico against the Kickapoos. Although he did not cross into Mexico with Mackenzie, Shafter performed valuable service for the expedition. He provided important information on the Mexican population, the location of villages, and the whereabouts of Mexican troops. Mackenzie stated that he was under great obligation to Shafter for his cordial cooperation and active support throughout the 1873 expedition.[19]

In 1875, after a lengthy stint in New York to study infantry equipment, Shafter led a huge command of African American troops for six months on the Staked Plains of West Texas and Eastern New Mexico. The Llano Estacado campaign, it was called, proved grueling. At one stretch during the wearisome expedition Shafter in ten days marched his men nearly three hundred miles. Since they were seldom in camp for more than one night, the men, in addition to marching thirty miles a day, had to pack their tents and other field equipment each morning and unpack it again each night. The subsequent wear and tear on both men and animals prompted one officer to complain that "our horses will go to the devil very fast at the rate Col. Shafter charges the whole command. . . ."[20]

The comment could not have been more pointed. In the field Shafter demonstrated an unsurpassed ability to get the utmost out of his soldiers. During the agonizing 1875 expedition, in which his command covered over 2500 miles of the High Plains, many of Shafter's men returned from the first crossing of the

Plains without shirts or shoes, most were missing some article of clothing, and all were exhausted. Nevertheless, only two weeks later, Shafter started back across the Plains again, and hardly had he completed the second crossing when a third was commenced. The Llano Estacado campaign was as successful as it was difficult. It swept the Plains clear of Indians, destroyed completely the dreary myth of the Plains as the dreaded Sahara of North America, and paved the way for settlement which quickly followed.[21]

Even more arduous and successful, was Shafter's 1876 expedition to the mouth of the Pecos River. Three times during the strenuous, five-months long campaign, Shafter marched his well-disciplined black troops across the rugged Coahuila deserts of Mexico. In each instance the troops rode in over 100° heat, and on one occasion they went sixty-five miles through the parching desert without water. During the summer his men twice engaged and defeated Indians. Two large camps of hostiles were completely destroyed, another in the Carmen Mountains was discovered and its location noted, 137 horses and mules and much stolen stock were recovered, and an estimated eighteen Indians were killed or captured.[22]

Shortly after the close of the Pecos River expedition, Shafter became commander of the District of the Nueces. Embracing the upper Rio Grande border area from Laredo to old Fort Leaton, the region was a natural haunt and even a highway for roving bands of Lipan and Mescalero Apaches who slipped across the Rio Grande to prey upon the abundant cattle and horse herds along the upper reaches of the Nueces. Any luckless cowboy or traveler who got in their way, the Indians killed. One raid in 1878 resulted in the death of eighteen citizens, including some women and children.[23]

Protecting the Rio Grande frontier was no easy task. Not only was the topography of the territory on both sides of the river barren and waterless, but Mexican troops resented the presence of American soldiers south of the border. As a result relations between the United States and Mexico were strained and Mexican leaders protested each American violation of their country's soil. Moreover, by criticizing the border crossings Democratic leaders in Washington hoped to embarrass the Rutherford B. Hayes administration. Consequently, Lieutenant Colonel Shafter needed to act with astute diplomatic good will and with the consummate skill demanded of desert campaigning.

Shafter was not timid in his new task. The audacious commander kept his bluecoats in the field. Small patrols suffered through December's cold, scouting relentlessly each trail and vigilantly watching for evidence of raiding parties from Mexico. The perseverance paid dividends. In January 1877, after some marauders were seen, Shafter from his headquarters at Fort Clark quickly dispatched Lt. John L. Bullis of his regiment and Capt. Alexander B. Keyes, Tenth Cavalry, and over one hundred officers and men some 125 miles deep into the Santa Rosa Mountains of Mexico. The Bullis-Keyes raid recovered much stolen stock and led to the return of several horses and mules.[24]

Additional border crossings followed. In March Shafter waded the Rio Grande with a large detachment of black troops, but too late to rescue from jail two men, who had guided his troops the year previous, sentenced to die as traitors. In July, Bullis splashed across the river, but with little luck in striking Indians or recovering stolen stock. In the fall, as raiding increased, Shafter twice directed well-armed expeditions to pursue hostile Indians to their sanctuaries in Mexico.[25]

Indeed, Shafter took personal command of the first expedition. The raid into Mexico began near the end of September after black scouts reported to Bullis, scouting along the Rio Grande near the mouth of Las Moras Creek, that marauders had entered Texas. Bullis immediately sent word by courier to Shafter at Fort Clark. In turn the district commander ordered the scrappy lieutenant with his force of ninety men to cross the river on the twenty-eighth and wait for Shafter who, with about three hundred troops of the Eighth and Tenth cavalries, was on his way to join him. When he rode into camp about 2:00 P.M. the same day,

Shafter ordered Bullis to start after dark for the Indian village near Saragosa. He promised to protect Bullis' rear in the event that there were wounded soldiers who might slow the retreating command. Both officers were well aware that a Mexican force of some two hundred soldiers, as well as dozens of thieves and desperadoes in the vicinity, would be watching for a favorable opportunity to strike the exhausted invaders.

About 11:00 P.M. Bullis started. Alternating his pace between a trot and a gallop during the long night ride, he reached Saragosa, about forty miles distant, at sunrise. Marching up Perdido Creek, he caught by surprise about 8:00 A.M. the Lipans and Mescaleros who fled for safety upon sighting the charging American troops. Bullis' scouts and troops chased the terrified Indians for four or five miles, capturing before reining to a halt four squaws, one boy, twelve horses, and two mules. After burning the small village and destroying the camp equipage, Bullis, turning his troops due north toward the head of the San Diego River where he was to meet Shafter, marched at a fast walk or trot until he reached the appointed rendezvous about 9:00 P.M. His troops, who had been in their saddles continuously for twenty-two hours, rolled from the horses in exhaustion. The support troops were no where in sight.

Meanwhile, Shafter had waited until morning before starting for the rendezvous. After moving slowly up the San Diego River, he encamped a few miles from its head. On the following morning, September 30, a little after sunrise, he spied Bullis, who had had an apprehensive, but undisturbed, night's rest, moving northeastward toward the Rio Grande and not far behind a column of approximately ninety Mexican troops from Saragosa under Col. Innocente Rodriguez. Immediately, he broke camp and joined his trusty subordinate.[26]

The combined command, nearly four hundred troops, continued toward the river at a brisk walk all day and late into the night. Colonel Rodriguez cautiously followed about a mile behind for a distance of ten miles, but then suddenly disappeared when Shafter began to maneuver his troops in preparation for battle.[27]

No engagement took place, nor were any shots fired, and, when Shafter again headed for the Rio Grande, some of the officers grumbled about running from "a handful of Mexicans."[28] After wading the river at Lasora Crossing near San Felipe about midnight, Shafter rested his command for two days before returning to Fort Clark, where he arrived on October 4.[29]

The raid brought unfavorable reaction in the capitals of both countries. In Mexico City, the newspapers, exaggerating its significance, indicated that the American troops had flagrantly violated international law. They also boasted of how a small Mexican force of only ninety troops had easily repelled an American force four times its number. In Washington, the raid became an important factor that influenced the decision of Congress to investigate the Texas border troubles.[30]

The Congressional investigations revealed the need for additional troops in the District of the Nueces.[31] Accordingly, in February 1878, when Col. Ranald Mackenzie arrived with his Fourth Cavalry, Shafter was relieved of his command. Still assigned to the district, however, he once again found himself closely teamed with his former colonel.

With adequate troops to end the depredations Shafter and Mackenzie wasted little time in bringing peace to the border. In April and May they planned and organized a major raid to destroy in Mexico hostile Indian lairs, and in June, with the army's approval, they carried it out. Twice during the bold assault there were confrontations, but not clashes, with Mexican troops who turned away after first challenging the Americans. Perhaps embarrassed that his troops had backed down in the face of the hated gringos, Porfiro Diaz, President of Mexico, took steps to cooperate with the United States in halting depredations north of the Rio Grande. Consequently, no further border crossings were necessary and by the end of 1878 tension along the river had relaxed demonstrably.[32]

Early the following year Shafter left Texas. In March his long awaited promotion to colonel came through and he was transferred to the First Infantry Regiment stationed in Dakota. He returned to Texas in late 1880 to pursue followers of Victorio, the marauding Apache. Later he moved to Arizona to help pacify Apache renegades. In 1891, following the Wounded Knee incident, he participated in the Siouan Campaign, and in 1898, during the Spanish-American War, he led the American Expeditionary force to Cuba.

The techniques of command vary, of course, with the personality of the commander. While some men prefer to lead by suggestion or example or other methods, Shafter chose to drive his subordinates by bombast and by threats, and he believed that profanity was the most convincing medium of communication. Although his mannerisms achieved spectacular results, they did not win affection among his men. Good-humored, even jolly, in his intimate personal relationships, he was likely to give short, blunt answers to his subalterns, he would never allow his orders to be challenged, and he always demanded the same dogged determination from his men that he himself gave to field maneuvers.

Clearly, as a commander of black troops in West Texas, the volatile Shafter was tough and aggressive. Energetic, resourceful, and courageous, he possessed initiative, looked out for the welfare of his men and animals, and was utterly unafraid of responsibility. When he thought that they were not being treated properly, he vociferously defended his African American soldiers, and he always spoke highly of their ability. Most officers learned to like him and his men, although he rarely enjoyed their affection, who always remembered him as a zealous, and forceful commander.

NOTES

1. Capt. Theodore A. Baldwin, Tenth Cavalry, to his wife, August 1875, in L.F. Sheffy, ed., "Letters and Reminiscences of Gen. Theodore A. Baldwin: Scouting after Indians on the Plains of Texas," *Panhandle Plains Historical Review,* XI (1938), 7-30 (hereafter cited as Baldwin, "Letters and Reminiscences).

2. William G. Muller, *The Twenty-fourth Infantry, Past and Present* (n.p., 1928), 1-8.

3. Ibid.; and Baldwin, "Letters and Reminiscences," 7-30.

4. Returns from Regular Army Infantry Regiments June 1821-December 1961 (Regimental Returns). Forty-first Infantry, February 1867, Microcopy No. 665, Roll 296, National Archives (NA).

5. James Parker, *The Old Army; Memories, 1872-1918* (Philadelphia: Dorrence & Co., 1929), 100.

6. Post Medical Reports, Fort Concho, January 1870, Book No. 401-3-4-7, December 1867-June 1889, Old Records Division (ORD), Adjutant Generals Office (AGO), NA.

7. Ibid., February 1870.

8. William R. Shafter to H. Clay Wood, Assistant Adjutant General, Department of Texas, October 10, 1870, Post Records, Fort McKavett, Record Group (RG) 393, NA, in Jerry Sullivan, ed., "Lieutenant Colonel W.R. Shafter's Pecos River Expedition of 1870," *West Texas Historical Association Year Book* XLVII (1971), 149-53.

9. Shafter to Wood, July 15, 1871, Letters Sent, Fort Davis, United States Army Command, (USAC), RG 98, NA; Post Medical Reports, Fort Davis, June-July 1871, Book No. 7-9-12, ORD, AGO, NA; Returns from U.S. Military Posts, 1800-1916 (Post Returns) Fort Davis, June-July 1871, Microcopy No 617, Roll 297, NA; J. Evetts Haley, *Fort Concho and the Texas Frontier* (San Angelo, Tex.: San Angelo *Standard Times,* 1952), 161-67.

10. Shafter to Wood, July 15, 1871, LS, Fort Davis, USAC, RG 98, NA.

11. Shafter to Wood, January 4, 1872 and February 1, 1872, LS, Fort Davis, USAC, RG 98, NA; Post Returns, Fort Davis, October 1871, Microcopy No. 617, Roll 297, NA.

12. Shafter to Wood, January 4, 1872 and February 1, 1872, LS, Fort Davis, USAC, RG 98, NA; Post Returns, Fort Davis, October 1871, Microcopy No. 617, Roll 297, NA; Post Medical Reports, Fort Davis, October-November 1871, Book No. 7-9-12, ORD, AGO, NA.

13. Shafter to Lt. Isaiah H. McDonald, Ninth Cavalry, December 8, 1871, in Shafter to Wood, January 4, 1872, LS, Fort Davis, USAC, RG 98, NA.

14. Shafter to F.C. Taylor, Agent, El Paso Mail Lines, ca. January 4, 1872, LS, Fort Davis, USAC, RG 98, NA.

15. Ibid.; Arlen Fowler, *The Black Infantry in the West* (Westport, Conn.: Greenwood Publishing Corporation, 1971), 25-26.

16. Shafter to S.R. Miller, Justice of the Peace, Presidio County, November 6, 1871, LS, Fort Davis, USAC, RG 98, NA.

17. A.J. Evans, Brief for the Appellees, Presidio Mining Co. *v.* Alice Bullis, Supreme Court of Texas, Austin Term, 1887 (filed with 2220 Appointments, Commissions, and Personal (ACP) 1879, Letters Received (LR), AGO, RG 94, NA; David S. Stanley, Commanding the Department of Texas, to Adjutant General, United States Army, July 2, 1887 (filed with 2220 ACP 1879), LR, AGO, RG 94, NA.

18. Shafter, "Report of Scout," July 22, 1872, and Wentz C. Miller, "Report of Scout," September 2, 1872, in Ernest Wallace, *Ranald S. Mackenzie's Official Correspondence Relating to Texas, 1871-1873* (Lubbock: West Texas Museum Association, 1967), 101.

[19.] General Orders No. 6, Department of Texas, June 2, 1873, in Shafter Papers, Stanford University Library, Stanford, California (photocopies in Southwest Collection, Texas Tech University, Lubbock); Ernest Wallace, *Ranald S. Mackenzie on the Texas Frontier* (Lubbock: West Texas Museum Association, 1964), 92-114.

[20.] Baldwin, "Letter and Reminiscences," 7-10.

[21.] Shafter to J.H. Taylor, Assistant Adjutant General, Department of Texas, January 4, 1876, 4688 AGO 1876, LR, RG 94, NA. In 1876 Charles Goodnight trailed a large cattle herd from Colorado southeastward into Palo Duro Canyon.

[22.] Shafter to Taylor, June 20, 1876, in Shafter Papers; Shafter and Lt. John L. Bullis, Twenty-fourth Infantry, Testimony before House Committee on Military Affairs, January 6-8, l878; "Texas Border Troubles," 45 Con., 2 Sess., *House Misc. Doc.* 64, 154-90; Paul H. Carlson., "William R. Shafter: Military Commander in the American West" (unpublished Ph.D. dissertation, Texas Tech University, Lubbock, 1971), 180-219.

[23.] Capt. John O. Elmore, Twenty-fourth Infantry, to Acting Assistant Adjutant General, District of the Rio Grande, Fort Brown, May 23, 1878, 4584 AGO 1878 (filed with 1653 AGO 1875), Affairs on the Rio Grande and Texas, LR 1805,-89, NA.

[24.] Bullis, Testimony before House Committee on Military Affairs, January 8, 1878, as cited, 188-90; Post Returns, Fort Clark, January 1877, Microcopy No. 617, Roll 214, NA.

[25.] Taylor to Shafter, April 1, 1877, Taylor to Brig. Gen. Edward O.C. Ord, Commanding Department of Texas, April 5, 1877, Shafter to Taylor, October 1, 1877, and Shafter to Ord, December 24, 1877, in Shafter Papers; Fowler, *The Black Infantry in the West*, 34-35; Shafter and Bullis, Testimony before House Committee on Military Affairs, January 6-8, 1878, as cited, 154-90.

[26.] Bullis, Testimony before the House Committee on Military Affairs, January 8, 1878, as cited, 191; Shafter to Taylor, October 1, 1877 in Shafter Papers; Bullis to Helenus Dodt, Twenty-fourth Infantry, Post Adjutant at Fort Clark, October 12, 1877, in Shafter Papers.

[27.] Bullis, Testimony before the House Committee on Military Affairs, January 8, 1878, as cited, 19l- 93; Shafter to Taylor, October 1, 1877, Shafter to Ord, December 24, 1877, and Bullis to Dodt, October 12, 1877, in Shafter Papers; also see J. Fred Rippy, *The United States and Mexico* (rev. ed. New York: F. S. Crofts and Company, 1931), 294-95.

[28.] Second Lt. Edward P. Turner, Tenth Cavalry, Testimony before the House Committee on Military Affairs, March 2, 1878, as cited, 269.

[29.] Post Returns, Fort Clark, October 1877, Microcopy No. 617, Roll 214, NA.

[30.] "Report and Accompanying Documents of the Committee on Relations of the United States with Mexico," 45 Cong., 2 Sess., *House Report* 701, 21-30; J.M. Callahan, *American Foreign Policy in Mexican Relations* (New York: The Macmillan Company, 1932), 190-93; Rippy, *The United States and* Mexico, 285-300; Chester L. Barrows, *William M. Evarts, Lawyer, Diplomat, Statesman* (Chapel Hill: University of North Carolina Press, 1941), 351-61.

[31.] General Orders No. 7 District of the Nueces, June 11, 1878, in Shafter Papers; Mackenzie to Assistant Adjutant General, Department of Texas, June 21, 1878, in Wallace, *Ranald Mackenzie's Official Correspondence*, 204-209; Wallace, *Ranald Mackenzie on the Texas Frontier*, 176-79.

Second Lieutenant Henry O. Flipper
A Black Officer on the West Texas Frontier

Paul H. Carlson

When Henry Ossian Flipper graduated from West Point and received his commission as a second lieutenant in the Tenth Cavalry, he became not only the first member of his race to graduate from the United States Military Academy, but also the first African American officer in the Regular United States Army. From 1878 to 1882 Lieutenant Flipper served at various frontier posts in the Southwest and participated in the campaign against Victorio and his band of Apaches. His military career ended prematurely in 1882, however, when a court-martial at Fort Davis, Texas, convicted him of conduct unbecoming an officer and a gentleman and sentenced him to be dismissed from the service. In spite of the guilty verdict, Flipper maintained his innocence to his death in 1940 and claimed he had been the victim of a conspiracy headed by Col. William R. Shafter, his commanding officer.[1]

The first of five sons,² Flipper was "born to Isabella and Festus Flipper on March 21, 1856, in Thomasville, Georgia."³ Prior to 1859, Isabella and her son belonged to Rev. Reuben H. Lucky, a Methodist preacher in Thomasville, while Festus was the property of Ephriam G. Ponder, a respected slave-dealer. In spite of his status as a slave, Flipper's father earned a comfortable living as a shoemaker and carriage trimmer, and eventually he purchased his wife and son from Lucky. Shortly after the Flipper family was united, Ponder took them to Atlanta.⁴

Flipper's education began when he was eight years old. He attended night classes which met in a woodshop. Following a brief interruption by the Civil War, he resumed his education in a "private" school run by a neighbor woman. In 1866 he and his younger brother, Joseph, transferred to a formal school operated by the American Missionary Association. When the association opened the Storrs' School in the following year, the Flipper boys transferred once again. In 1869 they began attending Atlanta University and four years later, while still a student there, Henry Flipper received his appointment to the United States Military Academy at West Point. Republican James Crawford Freeman from the Fifth Congressional District of Georgia had nominated him for the position.⁵

After passing the required examinations, Flipper became a cadet on July 1, 1873, at the age of seventeen years and four months.⁶ He spent the next four years surrounded by fellow cadets who were officially friendly, but socially aloof. His relationship with the faculty was somewhat different. He spoke highly of his professors, since they were always willing to provide aid and assistance whenever asked.⁷ When graduation day arrived on June 14, 1877, Flipper stood fiftieth in a class of seventy-sixth.⁸ He officially became a second lieutenant the following day, and he asked for and received an assignment with the Tenth United States Cavalry. General Orders 61 assigned Lieutenant Flipper to Company A, stationed at Fort Concho, Texas.⁹

Before Flipper could join his new company in Texas, however, it had been transferred to Fort Sill, Indian Territory, and it was to this post that the lieutenant reported for active duty on January 1, 1878.[10] While stationed there, Flipper met a young woman who had a significant effect on his life.

When Capt. Nicholas Nolan, Flipper's company commander, brought his new bride, the former Annie Dwyer, to Fort Sill, they were accompanied by Mrs. Nolan's sister Mollie. Miss Dwyer, like her sister, was Irish and very pretty. Immediately after they settled in their quarters, Annie Nolan insisted that Flipper board with them, which he promptly began to do after releasing his own cook. Before long a strong bond of friendship developed between Henry and Mollie, and they spent hours at a time riding horses and chasing jackrabbits and coyotes.[11]

In February 1879, Flipper and his company received orders transferring them to Fort Elliott, Texas, at present Mobeetie. They remained at this post until November when they were sent back to Fort Sill. Within six months Company A was on the move once again. This time it had been ordered, along with two other companies, to proceed via Fort Griffin to Fort Concho, Texas.[12]

Lieutenant Flipper's company left Fort Sill on May 25, 1880, and after being slowed by flooded rivers and heavy rains reached Fort Concho twenty-two days later.[13] The arrival of Flipper and his fellow cavalrymen on June 16 created some excitement in the post's neighboring settlement of Saint Angela, as the *Concho Weekly Times* noted:

> The town was considerably enlivened Wednesday by the arrival of three companies of the 10th Calvary, Company A, Captain Nolan; Company G, Captain Lee; and Company I, Captain Baldwin. The second officer of Company A is Lieutenant Flipper, the first and only colored man who ever graduated from West Point, and the only colored man who today holds a commission in the U.S. regular army.[14]

Special Orders Number 136 officially assigned the men to duty at Fort Concho, but they were hardly there long enough to unpack their belongings. Company A left the post on June 29, less than two weeks after its arrival, for a three-month campaign against hostile Indians raiding along the Rio Grande.[15]

During his brief stay at Fort Concho, Flipper had dined on occasion with the post commander, Col. Benjamin H. Grierson, who was also the organizer and present commander of the Tenth Cavalry. Grierson was highly impressed by Flipper's soldierly bearing and gentlemanly conduct, and when the lieutenant later ran into problems at Fort Davis, became one of his staunchest supporters.[16]

The Indians who brought Lieutenant Flipper and his company into the field were none other than Victorio and his band of Apaches. The trouble, which had begun in 1877, had become acute in April 1879, when the Chiricahua warrior led his followers in the first of many devastating raids through New Mexico, southwestern Texas, and northern Mexico.[17] After numerous long and exhaustive pursuits failed to capture the wily Apaches, Grierson decided on a defensive strategy. He would use his Tenth Cavalry troopers to block Victorio's access to water and thereby cause the Indian's ultimate defeat.

The colonel's strategy was difficult to implement, however, for there were more passes, crossings, and scattered water holes than his troops could effectively defend at one time. To accomplish his objective, Colonel Grierson had to anticipate Victorio's subsequent moves and take prompt action to intercept him. To put his plan in motion Grierson ordered Companies A, G, and I to leave Fort Concho and take up appropriate stations in the field.[18]

Flipper and his company proceeded to Fort Stockton, Texas, where they remained for four days. They then marched to Musquiz Canyon, near Fort Davis, and set up camp to await further orders. These orders came on July 20, 1880. Word had been received that Victorio was heading toward Eagle Springs, Texas. Consequently, the colonel ordered Company A to Fort Quitman, Texas, an abandoned post on the Rio Grande, while he went to Eagle Springs. Upon arriving at his destination, Grierson learned that the Apaches were still in Mexico. Expecting the flooded Rio Grande and Mexican troops under Colonel Valle to prevent Victorio from crossing into Texas, Colonel Grierson moved to Fort Quitman. Unfortunately, Grierson's expectations were unfulfilled, and he was forced to return at once to Eagle Springs in an effort to intercept the Indians, whom he was certain had crossed the river by now.[19]

On the way, the colonel received confirmation that Victorio was indeed in Texas. This news was relayed from Eagle Springs where Flipper and two men had ridden ninety-eight miles in twenty-two hours to deliver it. According to Flipper, he felt no ill effects from the ride until he attempted to dismount and tumbled to the ground. Unable to rise, he had his saddle blanket spread beside him and rolled over on it. He then had his saddle placed beneath his head to serve as a pillow and spent the remainder of the night in this position. When the bright sun woke him the following day, Flipper returned to Fort Quitman.[20]

Flipper's next involvement with Victorio came during the Battle of Tinaja de los Palmas, fifteen miles west of Eagle Springs. The fight, which took place on July 30, lasted almost four hours. Although Lieutenant Flipper and Company A failed to arrive until the closing moments of the battle, their addition to the conflict forced the Indians to withdraw toward the Rio Grande. According to his memoirs, this brief encounter with the retreating Apaches was the only time Flipper ever came under fire. When the dust had settled, the troopers were left with one dead and one wounded. Flipper read the Episcopal service and then took charge of the detail which buried the slain cavalryman where they had fallen.[21]

Except for a minor encounter at Rattlesnake Springs on August 6, the remainder of Flipper's service in the Victorio War was spent on scouts and patrols. Lieutenant Flipper searched among the various passes and ravines of the trans-Pecos mountains, where he found numerous signs to indicate that the Indians were in the area, but the Apaches themselves were never seen. Following a lightning raid on a stagecoach on August 19,

Victorio crossed into Mexico and took refuge in the Candelaria Mountains. A few days later Company A moved back to Fort Quitman.[22]

Lieutenant Flipper spent the next two months, and most of the third, at this location, scouting and patrolling along the Rio Grande. With the Apaches in Mexico, however, this duty took on a routine nature. As it turned out, Victorio never menaced Texas again, for word arrived on October 24 that he had been killed during an attack on his camp by the Chihuahua State Militia under Col. Joaquin Terrazas. News of the Apache warrior's death momentarily broke the monotony at Fort Quitman, but it failed to alter the situation of the troops there. Although orders on October 11 had transferred Company A to Fort Davis, it was November 25 before it actually started for its new post.[23]

After a four-day march, Flipper and his company reached Fort Davis and reported for duty on November 29, 1880. They spent the following day establishing themselves in their quarters, storing equipment, and familiarizing themselves with the post. By December 1, Company A and its officers were settled in their new home and performing the usual garrison duties. For the enlisted men, this included such assignments as stable police, kitchen detail, guard duty, and a number of other rotating fatigue or labor details. For the officers, it meant being assigned to special duties such as post adjutant, post engineer, or post signal officer. Lieutenant Flipper unfortunately received the most nightmarish assignment of all; effective December 1, he became Acting Assistant Quartermaster and Acting Commissary of Subsistence.[24]

As post quartermaster and commissary, Flipper became the most "popular" man on the post—at least when someone needed something. His duties included everything from "supplying a hinge for a corral gate to cleaning dead pigeons out of the post's water supply. He was expected to solve any and all problems pertaining to transportation, carpentry, painting, masonry, feed, forage, and plumbing."[25] He was in constant demand by the post commander who wanted to know about missing estimates, requisitions, and reports. Company commanders complained about the rations he issued to their men, and the wives who lived at the post constantly returned items he sold them from the commissary. Poor Flipper—maybe if he had not been so efficient in the field he would not have been elevated to such a "sublime" position. In spite of such headaches, however, Flipper fulfilled his obligation to the best of his ability and apparently complained very little about the difficulty of his job.[26]

The rest of December and the first half of January were relatively uneventful. Flipper received orders to "shoot one public mule," and a board of survey met on January 14, 1881, to investigate some damaged commissary stores, but these were merely routine matters. Even New Years had been uneventful. Flipper wrote in his memoirs that only one officer came to see him that day.[27]

About the middle of January, Flipper's life suddenly changed. Charles Berger, the post guide, failed to return to the post from a ten-day leave that began on December 30, causing Flipper a great deal of concern. He was worried about the guide's absence, because the latter had taken some property that Henry was accountable for. When a letter to Fort Concho failed to locate Berger, Lieutenant Flipper reported him as missing and asked for a board of survey to relieve him of any responsibility for the "stolen" items. The board met on February 18 and after a thorough investigation into the matter recommended that the lieutenant be absolved of any guilt and that the guide be charged with theft of government property.[28]

This business with Berger had broken the monotony, but the latter part of February proved to be even more exciting. One afternoon, as he was finishing his dinner, Flipper noticed flames shooting from one of the stacks of hay used to feed the horses. Dashing from his quarters, he ordered the fire alarm sounded and began a frantic attempt to save the hay. A bucket brigade passed water to Flipper who threw it on the burning stack as fast as he received it, but it was late that night before the fire was extinguished. Although the original stack was a total loss, several others nearby had been saved.

When the commotion finally ended, Flipper was soaking wet and nearly frozen stiff. The water he had thrown on the burning hay had run down the sides and into his boots, where it froze. As a result of spending several hours in this condition, Flipper soon found himself sick in his quarters and under close medical supervision. Reportedly, he was suffering from an attack of typhoid malarial fever which he had contracted at Fort Sill. Since the medicine for the treatment had been used in the field, the post surgeon administered some morphine nightly. Flipper finally responded to treatment and shortly after the first of the month was able to resume his normal duties.[29]

Things ran smoothly for almost a week, and then something more serious happened. Col. William R. Shafter, First Infantry, replaced Maj. Napoleon B. McLaughlen as post commander at Fort Davis on March 12, 1881. Shafter was no newcomer to Fort Davis, nor was he a stranger to the Tenth Cavalry. As commander of the Twenty-fourth Infantry, he had commanded the post in the early 1870s, and in 1875 he led an expedition including six companies of the Tenth onto the unexplored Staked Plains. This was his first contact with Lieutenant Flipper, however, and from the first a feeling of animosity seems to have developed.[30]

Immediately upon assuming command of the garrison, one of Shafter's first official acts was to relieve Lieutenant Flipper as Acting Assistant Quartermaster and to inform him that as soon as a suitable replacement could be found he would be removed as Acting Commissary of Subsistence. No reason was given for this hasty decision, and Flipper must have wondered why the new commander was eager to replace him. Perhaps the colonel simply wanted to fill these positions with men from his own regiment. Nevertheless, Flipper's civilian friends cautioned him to beware of Shafter, and the lieutenant did make a sincere effort to avoid trouble.[31]

Perhaps it was just as well that Flipper was busily occupied with official matters. His personal affairs had recently taken a downward turn, and for a time he had thought of little else. The trouble centered around Lt. Charles E. Nordstrom who had joined Company A at Fort Quitman. Although Mollie Dwyer was nothing more to Flipper, he claimed, than a close friend and riding companion, he jealously cherished her friendship as a welcome reprieve from his otherwise lonely existence. When Nordstrom joined the company, this relationship changed.

Mollie found less and less time to go riding with Flipper and devoted more and more of her afternoons to Nordstrom. Flipper became bitterly resentful of Nordstrom. The situation worsened when the two officers were forced to share quarters. Ordinarily, Flipper would have had periodic field assignments to relieve his "torment," but his special duty detained him at the post. Since Shafter's arrival, nothing seemed to go right.[32]

In spite of Lieutenant Flipper's effort to avoid trouble, his handling of the post commissary funds prompted Colonel Shafter on August 10, 1881, to relieve Henry as Acting Commissary of Subsistence. This was, of course, Shafter's prerogative. His next move certainly was not. He arrested Flipper for alleged embezzlement and placed him in the guardhouse, a serious violation of military protocol. Officers under arrest were usually restricted to quarters pending their trial, but they were never placed in a cell. Only rarely were they even placed under guard. The colonel's action not only surprised the personnel at Fort Davis, but it brought immediate orders from Department of Texas commander, Gen. C.C. Augur, for Lieutenant Flipper's release. Both the Secretary of War and the General of the Army concurred. Although Shafter removed Flipper from the guardhouse on August 16, the young officer's troubles had just begun. He faced a court-martial on charges of embezzlement.[33]

The court-martial which finally got under way on November 1 and lasted for over a month is the subject of another article.[34] But briefly, it was marked by such things as attempts to add new members after the court was sworn in and by petty arguments between the judge advocate and Flipper's defense counsel. The prosecution introduced a number of witnesses and tried to prove that Lieutenant Flipper was guilty of embezzling over $1,000 in government funds. The defense based its case on the premise that Flipper had already suffered enough abuse and should not be subjected to any more. It also pointed out that the government had not actually lost any money since a number of Flipper's friends had contributed the necessary amount to replace the missing funds.

The court found Lieutenant Flipper innocent of embezzlement but guilty of conduct unbecoming an officer and a gentleman and sentenced him to be dismissed from the service. After being reviewed by the proper authorities and approved by President Chester A. Arthur, the sentence took effect on June 30, 1882. Just four years after his celebrated graduation from West Point, Henry Ossian Flipper's military career came to an inglorious end.[35]

His life did not end there, however, for he refused to wallow in self pity. Instead he made himself a new career as one of the Southwest's leading civil engineers. Flipper even spent one year as an assistant to the Secretary of the Interior.[36] Though dismissed in disgrace, an African American had broken the color line to serve as a commissioned officer in the army of the United States and afterwards had gone on to achieve success in several other fields of endeavor.

NOTES

1. Wesley A. Brown, "Eleven Men of West Point," *The Negro History Bulletin*, XIX (April, 1956), 149; Theodore D. Harris, ed., *Negro Frontiersman: The Western Memoirs of Henry O. Flipper, First Negro Graduate of West Point* (El Paso: Texas Western College Press, 1963), vii; William H. Leckie, *The Buffalo Soldiers: A Narrative of the Negro Cavalry in the West* (Norman: University of Oklahoma Press, 1967), 237-38.

2. "Henry Ossian Flipper," *Journal of Negro History*, XXV (July, 1940), 403.

3. Henry Ossian Flipper, *The Colored Cadet at West Point* (New York: Arno Press and the New York Times, 1969), i. Originally published in 1878, this autobiography provides an entertaining account of Flipper's experiences at West Point.

4. Ibid., 7-8; Brown, "Eleven Men of West Point," 148. Festus did not actually own his wife and children himself. He had "loaned" the money to Ponder so that he could buy them. There is no record, however, of the money ever being repaid. Ezra J. Warner, "A Black Man in the Long Gray Line," *American History Illustrated*, IV (January 1970), 30.

5. Flipper, *Colored Cadet*, 11-20; Brown, "Eleven Men of West Point," 148.

6. United States Military Academy, "Henry Ossian Flipper's Academic Record While a Cadet at The United States Military Academy, 1 July 1873-74 June 1877" (Xerox copy obtained by the author from Dr. William C. Mieher, San Angelo, Texas).

7. Flipper, *Colored Cadet*, 121, 321-22.

8. United States Military Academy, "Flipper's Academic Record."

9. George W. Cullum, *Biographical Register of the Officers and Graduates of the United States Military Academy at West Point, New York* (Xerox copy of extracts pertaining to Flipper obtained by the author from Dr. William C. Mieher, San Angelo, Texas); *New York Times*, June 28, 1877; Organizational Returns, Tenth Cavalry, June-December, 1877 (Microfilm of MSS in Fort Concho Museum, San Angelo, Texas).

10. Flipper, *Colored Cadet*, 33; Fort Sill, I.T., Post Returns, January 1878 (Microfilm of MSS property of the author); Fort Sill, I.T., Post Medical Records, January 1, 1878, 227 (Xerox copy of MSS in Fort Sill Museum, Fort Sill, Oklahoma).

11. Harris, *Negro Frontiersman*, 2-3. Flipper contended that this relationship with Mollie was strictly platonic.

12. Organizational Returns, Tenth Cavalry, February 1879-May 1880.

13. Ibid., May-June, 1880; Fort Sill, Post Returns, May 1880; Fort Sill, Post Medical Records, May 25 1880, 352; Fort Concho, Texas, Post Returns, June 1880 (Microfilm of MSS in Fort Concho Museum, San Angelo, Texas); U.S. Secretary of War, "Annual Report of 1880," 46 Cong., 3 sess., House Ex Doc. 1, pt. 2, 128; Harris, *Negro Frontiersman*, 15.

14. *Concho Weekly Times*, June 19, 1880. The town became known as San Angelo sometime after 1881. Leckie, *Buffalo Soldiers*, 235.

15. Special Orders No. 136, Headquarters, Department of Texas, July 9, 1880, Fort Concho, Post Returns, June 1880; Special Orders No. 17, Headquarters, District of the Pecos, June 27, 1880, ibid.; Organizational Returns, Tenth Cavalry, June 1880; Letter, Maj. Anson Mills to Adjutant General, Military Division of the Missouri, July 13, 1880, Fort Concho, Texas, Letters Sent, 1876-1883 (Microfilm of MSS in Angelo State College Library, San Angelo, Texas); San Antonio *Daily Express*, July 11, 1880.

16. Dr. William C. Mieher, "Henry Ossian Flipper" (paper presented to the Tom Green County Historical Society, San Angelo, Texas, March, 1967), n.p.; Leckie, *Buffalo Soldiers*, 238.

17. Carlysle Graham Raht, *The Romance of Davis Mountains and Big Bend Country* (Texana Edition; Odessa, Tex.: Raht-books Company, Publishers, 1963), 261, 271; Barry Scobee, Fort Davis Texas, 1583-1960 (El Paso: Hill Printing Company, 1963), 113; Leckie, *Buffalo Soldiers*, 179-85, 215; Frank M. Temple, "Colonel Grierson in the Southwest," *Panhandle-Plains Historical Review*, XXX (1957), 48-50.

18. U.S. Secretary of War, "Annual Report of 1880," 159; Leckie, *Buffalo Soldiers*, 223; Carl Coke Rister, *The Southwestern Frontier, 1845-1881* (Cleveland: Arthur H. Clark Company, 1928), 203; Temple, "Colonel Grierson in the Southwest," 49-50.

19. U.S. Secretary of War, "Annual Report of 1880," 159; Fort Concho, Post Returns, June 1880; Organizational Returns, Tenth Cavalry, June-July, 1880; Letter, Col. B.H. Grierson to Gen. E.O.C. Ord, July 24, 1880, Adjutant General's Office, Letters Received, Papers Relating to Military Operations Against Chief Victorio's Band of Mescalero Apaches, 1879-1881, hereinafter cited as Papers Relating to Victorio (Microfilm of MSS property of the author); Frank M. Temple, "Col. B.H. Grierson's Victorio Campaign," *West Texas Historical Association Year Book*, XXXV (October 1959), 101; Robert K. Grierson, "Journal kept on the Victorio Campaign in 1880," 5-11, hereinafter cited as Grierson, "Journal" (Typed copy of MS loaned to the author by Frank M. Temple). Robert was Colonel Grierson's twenty-one year old son.

20. U.S. Secretary of War, "Annual Report of 1880," 159-60; Grierson, "Journal," 11-13; Harris, *Negro Frontiersman*, 16.

21. U.S. Secretary of War, "Annual Report of 1880," 160; Grierson, "Journal," 14-16; Organizational Returns, Tenth Cavalry, July 1880; Telegram, Gen. P.H. Sheridan to Adjutant General of the Army, August 2, 1880, Papers Relating to Victorio; Letter, Col. B.H. Grierson to Assistant Adjutant General of the Army, July 31 1880, Fort Concho, Texas, Letters Received, 1880-1882 (Microfilm of MSS in Angelo State College Library, San Angelo, Texas); E.L.N. Glass, *The History of the Tenth Cavalry, 1886-1921* (Tuscon: Acme Printing Company, 1921), 22; Robert M. Utley, *Fort Davis National Historic Site, Texas*, National Park Service Historical Handbook Series, No. 38 (Washington, D.C.: Government Printing Office, 1965), 42-43; Harris, *Negro Frontiersman*, 16-17; *New York Times*, August 4, 1880. This encounter is sometimes called the Battle of Quitman Canyon or the Battle of Eagle Springs.

22. Organizational Returns, Tenth Cavalry, August, 1880; Telegram, Gen. E.O.C. Ord to Adjutant General, Military Division of the Missouri, August 4, 1880, Papers Relating to Victorio; Telegram, Col. Edward Hatch to Assistant Adjutant General, Military Division of the Missouri, August 14, 1880, ibid.; Telegram, Gen. E.O.C. Ord to Adjutant General Military Division of the Missouri, August 25, 1880, ibid.; U.S. Secretary of War, "Annual Report of 1880," 160-62; *Galveston Daily News*, August 6, 12, 1880; *New York Times*, August 11, 1880; Grierson, "Journal," 19-23; Utley, *Fort Davis*, 44; Harris, *Negro Frontiersman*, 17.

23. Organizational Returns, Tenth Cavalry, August-November, 1880; Fort Concho, Post Returns, October, 1880; Special Orders No. 207, Headquarters, Department of Texas, October 11, 1880, ibid.; Letter, Capt. Nicholas Nolan to Capt. Lewis Johnson, September 30, 1880, Fort Concho, Texas, Endorsements Sent, 1880-1881, p. 105 (Microfilm of MSS in Angelo State College Library, San Angelo, Texas); Fort Davis, Texas, Post Returns, October, 1880 (Microfilm of MSS in Fort Davis, National Historic Site, Fort Davis, Texas); Letter, Col. Joaquin Terrazas to Col. George Buell, October 22, 1880, Papers Relating to Victorio; Letter, Juan Navarro, Charge d' affairs

ad interim of Mexico to W.M. Evarts, U.S. Secretary of State, October 30, 1880, ibid.; Grierson, "Journal," 40-41; *Galveston Daily News*, October 14, 1880; Harris, *Negro Frontiersman*, 19; Leckie, *Buffalo Soldiers*, 227-29.

[24.] Organizational Returns, Tenth Cavalry, November-December, 1880; Fort Davis, Post Returns, November-December, 1880; Fort Davis, Texas, Post Medical Records, November 29, 1880, p. 283 (Microfilm of MSS in Fort Davis National Historic Site, Fort Davis, Texas); Don Rickey, Jr., *Forty Miles a Day on Beans and Hay: The Enlisted Soldier Fighting the Indian Wars* (Norman: University of Oklahoma Press, 1963), 94; U.S. Secretary of War, "Annual Report of 1881," 47 Cong., 2 Sess., House Ex. Doc. 1, pt. 2, p. 249; Special Orders No. 107, Headquarters, Fort Davis, Texas, December 1, 1880, Fort Davis, Texas, Orders, Circulars, Memoranda, 1867-1891 (Microfilm of MSS in Fort Davis National Historic Site, Fort Davis, Texas) and Fort Davis, Texas, Quartermaster Records, Consolidated File Unarranged (Microfilm of MSS in Fort Davis National Historic Site, Fort Davis, Texas).

[25.] S.E. Whitman, *The Troopers: An Informal History of the Plains Cavalry, 1865-1890* (New York: Hastings House Publishers, 1962), 63.

[26.] Ibid.; W.S. Nye, *Carbine & Lance: The Story of Old Fort Sill* (Norman: University of Oklahoma Press, 1942), 288; Harris, *Negro Frontiersman*, 17-18.

[27.] Special Orders No. 121, Headquarters, Fort Davis, Texas, December 17, 1880, Fort Davis, Orders, Circulars, Memoranda, 1867-1891; Special Orders No. 9, Headquarters, Fort Davis, Texas, January 13, 1881, ibid.; Harris, *Negro Frontiersman*, 20.

[28.] Letter, Lt. H.O. Flipper to Post Adjutant, Fort Concho, Texas, January 12, 1881, Fort Concho, Letters Received, 1880-1882; Letter, Lt. Robert Smither to Lt. H.O. Flipper, January 17, 1881, Fort Concho, Texas, Letters Sent, 1878-1881, p. 139 (Microfilm of MSS in Angelo State College Library, San Angelo, Texas); Special Orders No. 31, Headquarters, Fort Davis, Texas, February 17, 1881, Fort Davis, Orders, Circulars, Memoranda, 1867-1891; Proceedings of a Board of Survey which convened at Fort Davis, Texas, pursuant to Special Orders No. 31 series 1881 of that post; Records Relating to the Army Career of Henry Ossian Flipper, 1873-1883, hereinafter cited as Flipper Records (Microfilm of MSS property of the author).

[29.] Harris, *Negro Frontiersman*, 18-19; Organizational Returns, Tenth Cavalry, February 1881; Fort Davis, Post Returns, February 1881.

[30.] Fort Davis, Post Returns, March 1881; Fort Davis, Texas, Post Medical Records, March 12, 1881, 287 (Microfilm of MSS in Fort Davis National Historic Site, Fort Davis, Texas); Utley, *Fort Davis*, 60; Francis B. Heitman, *Historical Register and Dictionary of the United States Army* (Urbana: University of Illinois Press, 1965), 876; Leckie, *Buffalo Soldiers*, 143. As a major general, Shafter became notorious during the Spanish-American War as the commander of the United States' Cuban expeditionary force. Robert M. Utley, "'Pecos Bill' on the Texas Frontier," *The American West* VI (January 1969), 4.

[31.] Special Order No. 50, Headquarters, Fort Davis, Texas, March 12, 1881, Fort Davis, Orders, Circulars, Memoranda, 1867-1891; Organizational Returns, Tenth Cavalry, March 1881; Fort Davis, Post Returns, March 1881; U.S. Secretary of War, "Annual Report of 1881," p. 249; Harris, *Negro Frontiersman*, 20.

[32.] Organizational Returns, Tenth Cavalry, May-July 1881; Fort Davis, Post Returns, May-July, 1801; Special Orders No. 109, Headquarters, Fort Davis, Texas, May 24, 1881, Fort Davis, Orders, Circulars, Memoranda, 1867-1891; Fort Davis, Post Medical Records, May 30, 1881, p. 299; ibid., July 11, 1881, p. 305; ibid., July 17, 1881, p. 309; Harris, *Negro Frontiersman*, 19. Lieutenant Nordstrom and Mollie Dwyer were married after Flipper's dismissal in 1882. Ibid.

³³· Special Orders No. 173, Headquarters, Fort Davis, Texas, August 10, 1881, Fort Davis, Orders, Circulars, Memoranda, 1867-1891; Organizational Returns, Tenth Cavalry, August 1881; Fort Davis, Post Returns, August 1881; Telegram, Col. William R. Shafter to Adjutant General, Department of Texas, August 13 1881, Flipper Records; Telegram, Thomas Vincent, Adjutant General, Department of Texas, to Commanding Officer, Fort Davis, August 16, 1881, ibid.; Letter, R.C. Drum, Adjutant General of the Army, to Gen. C.C. Augur, August 23, 1881, ibid.; Whitman, *Troopers*, 98-99.

³⁴· The author is presently working on an article dealing with the court-martial itself and hopes to have it ready for publication in the near future.

³⁵· *Proceedings of a General Court-Martial which met at Fort Davis, Texas, pursuant to Special Orders No. 108*, Headquarters, Department of Texas, September 3, 1881, Flipper Records. The transcript of the trial along with the accompanying exhibits totals almost 750 typed pages.

³⁶· Harris, *Negro Frontiersman*, 20-21; Cullum, *Biographical Register*, n.p.

Blacks in San Angelo
Relations Between Fort Concho and the City, 1875–1889

Patricia E. Gower

Reconstruction and military control ended in 1874 in Texas. This not only meant the withdrawal of federal forces from the eastern region of the state but also a badly-needed increase in the number of troops for the frontier. In 1875, Col. Benjamin Grierson arrived at Ft. Concho to command the Tenth Cavalry headquartered there. The fort was now completely garrisoned with black soldiers and their white officers. These troops would play a pivotal role in many of the decisive exploratory and punitive expeditions which would be launched from Ft. Concho.[1]

The resentments fostered by Reconstruction traveled with the waves of settlers coming to the frontier. Blacks in uniform often were viewed with dislike and distrust and were an easy target for those resentful of both federal occupation and support for black freedom. There were troublesome incidents involving black troops and white townspeople from the time that the first black soldier appeared in the west. White soldiers were also the brunt of civilian resentment at times. Fort Concho largely avoided friction in the early years due to the prolonged absences of a large part of the fort's population on extended scouts to control Indian problems.[2]

The lack of strong governmental control in Mexico at this time freed many Indians and bandits there to cross the border in search of livestock and then cross back to escape pursuit. The Indians from the Panhandle also continued to launch raids to replenish their supplies of livestock. Grierson sent out numerous parties of soldiers to try to control the violence and by 1876 had the permission of General Ord to cross the border in pursuit. Several incursions into Mexico were carried out by Colonel Shafter in command of Tenth Cavalry troops. These troops were often joined by Black Seminoles led by Lt. John Bullis and eventually these efforts resulted in a more active Mexican military presence and a reduction of raids across the border. These expeditions not only kept the soldiers out of the fort for long periods from 1876 through 1879, they also opened large areas of West Texas that had been previously unexplored. The black soldiers penetrated the Big Bend area and the uncharted plains of the Panhandle. As the mystery surrounding the plains was removed by the soldiers' efforts to chart them, settlers were increasingly encouraged to move there.[3]

San Angelo grew up directly as a result of the federal presence. Workers brought in to construct the fort buildings often settled permanently in the area and the fort proved to be a magnet for gamblers, prostitutes and others hoping to relieve the soldiers of their pay. Early descriptions of San Angelo are unanimous in finding it an unattractive collection of saloons, ramshackle dwellings and brothels. In 1876, journalist Nathaniel Taylor traveled through the area and put the population of the settlement at approximately one hundred. In his memoirs of his travels, he wrote that the townspeople consisted of Mexican and white men and prostitutes. Another traveler of that time saw the town as one of several groups of picket dwellings, saloons and "houses of ill fame." Norman Badger, the post chaplain from 1871-1875, called the settlement around Fort Concho a "cordon of drinking and gambling saloons and no law." Upon his arrival at Fort Concho, Col. Benjamin Grierson described the village in very similar terms in a letter to his wife, Alice.[4]

An important witness to both the growth of early San Angelo and the presence of blacks in the army was Maj. William Wedemeyer. Born in Germany in 1836, he emigrated with his parents to the United States when he was fourteen. With the beginning of the Civil War, he enlisted as a lieutenant in the Wisconsin infantry. His memoirs reveal a man convinced of his own superiority to the majority of the officers and civilians that he found when he arrived at Ft. Concho in December of 1880. He viewed San Angelo with distaste and commented disparagingly on its appearance and the unrulier elements of its population. He also disliked Benjamin Grierson and tended to place the blame for any problems that arose at the fort on his shoulders. He was unimpressed with black soldiers in the army but he did accept that their presence would in all likelihood continue and since this was the case, he supported their full citizenship and the right to vote since they could never be "educated and civilized" without these privileges. He believed that "darkies [were] natural thieves" but was forced to admit, on his arrival at Fort Concho, that he found them well disciplined and drilled and that his white troopers got along with them much better than he had expected.[5]

The fort's derisive name for the fledging San Angelo was "Over the River," and the soldiers' contempt was one cause of the resentment in San Angelo towards the fort which sometimes resulted in violent confrontations. Dr. William Notson, the first post surgeon, wrote that "St. Angela, the village across the North Concho . . . [had] achieved an unenviable distinction for numerous murders."[6] Grierson was distressed enough about the violence, especially that committed against troopers, to complain about it in official reports. Wedemeyer also commented on the unruliness of cowboys and other lawless elements, the frequency of murders in the town and the fear created by these conditions for the other townspeople. Alice Grierson wrote to her son Charles in December of 1875 that five men had been killed across the river in one week.[7]

The violent, unsavory and predatory nature of many of the inhabitants of a town like early San Angela contributed in a significant way to the friction between the soldiers and the civilians they were supposed to protect. Often, consumption of alcohol on both sides added to the tensions. Service life at Fort Concho was a primitive experience and the extreme isolation and boredom often contributed to excessive drinking. Fort Concho was typical of most frontier forts in the frequency that soldiers resorted to alcohol to relieve boredom and Dr. Notson believed that the "heavy sales of liquors [led] to increased lawlessness."[8]

Another serious problem that afflicted the soldiers in many frontier forts was venereal disease and Fort Concho was no exception to this pattern. At times, cases of venereal disease were the dominant illness in the post hospital and throughout the history of the fort, venereal disease continued to be a significant threat to the health of the troopers, black and white alike. Other serious diseases plagued frontier towns that lacked healthy water supplies and sanitary waste disposal. In 1881, Maj. William Wedemeyer made note of the fact that because of a smallpox outbreak in San Angelo, the fort had to be quarantined to avoid the spread of the disease to the fort personnel.[9]

Living conditions near the fort were not necessarily better than in town and improvements were often slow in coming. Clustered near the fort were the dwellings of the laundresses, prostitutes, and wives and mistresses of enlisted men. These camp followers lived mostly in tents and shacks with no sanitary facilities and were vulnerable to the flash floods common to the area. Finally in 1876, Grierson authorized the construction of some barracks north of the soldiers' quarters for the laundresses and other women and children but even at this time no privys were provided. About this time, with the help of Norman Badger, the Tenth Cavalry began construction of a chapel for blacks on the fort and in this small community who had despaired of never having one provided for their worship. This neighborhood grew as it attracted soldiers whose enlistment was up at Fort Concho and the other forts in the surrounding area. In West Texas, employment of any kind was scarce for blacks and the fort provided jobs as servants, cooks and stable hands. Many blacks were able to use skills learned in slavery to gain employment, but often these same skills confined them to the lower rungs of the employment ladder.[10]

In addition to the routine discrimination in employment and housing the blacks were exposed to, occasional clashes arose that were compounded of both racial bigotry and general animosity towards the military. There were two early incidents of this type involving both Texas Rangers and citizens of San Angelo in conflict with black soldiers of Fort Concho. In 1877, rangers abused some troopers in Nasworthy's saloon and then refused to apologize to Grierson. Just a short time later at Morris' saloon, a group of civilians cornered a soldier and ripped the insignia from his uniform. In both cases, the troopers went back to town with weapons and fired on the saloon killing bystanders.[11]

In 1881, Wedemeyer was a valuable eyewitness to the most serious outbreak of hostilities between the fort and the townspeople. Ironically, tensions seem to have arisen because of the killing of a white soldier. On January 19, Wedemeyer reported the death of a soldier in his company, one Private Pindar, who had been murdered by a gambler called Pleas Watson. He also reported that the sheriff, James Spear, was looking for Watson and that some of the citizens of San Angelo had offered a reward for his capture, probably in an attempt to avoid trouble with the fort. The San Antonio *Daily Express* recounted the murder on February 5, 1881, and also printed a report that Pleas Watson had been found in Gonzales City and arrested and that there seemed to be a "great deal of feeling" both in his favor and in support of the angry soldiers.[12]

A far more serious incident began shortly after this murder in the early morning of February 1st when a trooper of Co. E, Tenth Cavalry, named William Watkins was shot and killed in San Angelo. Major Wedemeyer again provided an invaluable account since his memoirs were likely to be disdainful but objective. He disliked Grierson, the black troopers and San Angelo equally and viewed the entire situation with an impartial distaste. He recounted that the man who was suspected of the killing was arrested by a sentry when he tried to cross the fort's perimeter. The post surgeon, Dr. Smith, confirmed that the ball in the dead man's head was the same weight as the ones found in the suspect's pistol. The suspect's name was reported both as Tom McCarty and McCarthy. Wedemeyer called him McCarty and believed him to be from Syracuse, New York.[13]

After Watkins' burial, all the men of Wedemeyer's company and many from other companies crossed the river and headed for town. One notable detail about this is that all the men in Wedemeyer's company were from the Sixteenth Infantry and thus were white. Wedemeyer discovered the absences and alerted the officer of the day and a patrol was sent to town to make the men return to the fort. Wedemeyer later learned that the men had arrested the sheriff at the Tankersley hotel and demanded that the prisoner be handed over to them but that McCarty had been hidden and could not be found. When Wedemeyer reported to Grierson, he received the impression that the colonel was not very worried and believed the men were justified in their action. Grierson did not order that an investigation be started or that any of the men involved be arrested.[14]

On February 4th, the sheriff and the prisoner came by the fort on the way to the jail in Ben Ficklin. Grierson sent a company to escort them and posted a sentry on the banks of the river to discourage both soldiers and the civilians from further hostilities. However, after dark, cowboys fired towards the sentry and the trouble erupted all over again. The cavalry troopers got their weapons and started for town. This time Wedemeyer's company of infantry was involved only in the effort to stop the cavalrymen. By the time Wedemeyer and his men reached San Angelo, around two hundred shots had been fired wildly into the houses and the soldiers had fled. Wedemeyer found a large number of extremely frightened civilians one of whom was slightly wounded. Roll was called to find out who was absent from the fort for this raid but most got back in time to answer. This time Wedemeyer reported that no white soldiers took part in the incident in the town. Three black non-commissioned officers were arrested and reduced in rank for their roles but no other action was taken.[15]

On the 6th of February, Wedemeyer found the situation much quieter and reported that a group of Texas Rangers had been brought in to keep the cowboys in line and guard the prisoner. His final comment on the matter was made on February 11. Grierson ordered him to prefer charges on the men of his company who took part in the first raid since he had arrested some of the blacks and believed the white soldiers should be punished as well. Wedemeyer was of the opinion that it was Grierson's fault that the whole thing happened at all. He blamed stupid remarks made within the hearing of the black troopers and "incendiary speeches" made by Grierson and other white officers and made no move to charge any of his men. Neither Wedemeyer nor Grierson had any sympathy with the civilians' outrage and both believed that the soldiers had been largely justified in their actions.[16]

Such incidents aroused a great deal of interest across the state. They were reported in the San Saba, San Antonio and Galveston papers but seemed to excite the most interest in the military town of San Antonio. There, details unreported in other papers and by Wedemeyer were covered in long stories often on the front page. Headlines seemed to be in sympathy with the soldiers at Fort Concho as they blared out "A Negro Soldier Shot in Cold Blood Without Any Apparent Cause," and "Fruitless Attempt of Soldiers to Take Revenge on the Murder of Their Comrade." The stories told of both of the most recent murders and announced that the soldiers were determined to put a stop to these attacks. The paper also reproduced a placard that the soldiers had distributed in town and also telegraphed to Military Headquarters. It read:

Fort Concho, Texas
February 3, 1881

We, soldiers of the US Army, do hereby warn, for the first and last time, all citizens, cowboys, etc. of San Angela and vicinity, to recognize our right-of-way as just and peaceable men. If we do not receive justice and fair play, which we must have, some one will suffer—if not the guilty, the innocent. It has gone far enough! Justice or death! US Soldiers.[17]

A second notice reported in the San Antonio paper threatened reprisals if McCarty was granted bail and a note to the sheriff threatened to destroy the town if McCarty were turned lose. The first foray into the town was reported to be made up of black and white soldiers but the paper added that the white soldiers had blackened their faces and encouraged the black soldiers by their talk. The paper also carried a report from McCarty from jail in Austin that the shooting was an accident that occurred during a scuffle and that he was a good friend with the black man who had been shot.[18]

In the May 3, 1924, anniversary issue of the San Angelo paper, the roots of the incident were reported to be the ill feelings between black soldiers and San Angelo and also between the town and Colonel Grierson. The black soldiers were portrayed as a "necessary evil" and arrogant in their dealings with the townspeople. The account at this time believed that incident would not have been noteworthy if the trooper had not been black since this fact alone distinguished it from many other such incidents. In relation to the confrontation at the Tankersley hotel, Mrs. Tankersley was portrayed as a heroine because of her role when she was confronted by the troopers who had arrested the sheriff and were searching for McCarty. The writer believed that Mrs. Tankersley saved McCarty from "probable torture and horrible death at the hands of the negro troops" by stalling for time as he was hurried out a back window. In place of Wedemeyer's view that the rangers were sent in to control the cowboys as well as the soldiers, the paper reported that they were present to control the federal troops and that the enmity between the town and the fort was of long standing. McCarty was thus simply following the earlier example of the buffalo hunters who often shot at black troopers on sight. As all views of the clash in San Angelo show, there was a sense of tension present in the early 1880's between the soldiers and the citizens. As expected, the military blamed the civilians while the civilians believed the fault lay with the federal troopers.[19]

Partly because of the friction between the town and the black soldiers, Grierson was ordered to shift the headquarters of the Tenth Cavalry to Fort Davis in July 1882. After this, the only black troops at Fort Concho were two companies of the Tenth Cavalry, E and F, which remained until March of 1885. The fort was garrisoned completely with white soldiers again but even then there was trouble in town for some of the men. Upon returning to San Angelo, Wedemeyer reported in 1886 that a soldier had his throat cut in the White Elephant Saloon, which was one of the saloons in town owned by black businessmen. There was some talk of an incident similar to the one in 1881 and reports to the sheriff that some soldiers were going to attempt to hang the prisoner but upon further investigation, no unusual absences were found and the situation cooled off.[20]

At the time he wrote this, Wedemeyer did see a great deal of improvement in San Angelo both in the buildings and the support of law and order that prevailed. The only reasons that he could find that any troopers were still at Fort Concho was that there were no quarters anywhere else for them. Despite his typically jaundiced view of things, it is evident that relations between

San Angelo and the fort had improved in the years between 1881 and 1886 and that many believed that the days of Fort Concho were numbered.[21]

The conclusion of the campaigns against the Indians in 1880 brought stability to the area and the presence of the fort was increasingly regarded by San Angelo as unnecessary. Although some disagreed, many in San Angelo called for the closing of the fort now that its protection was no longer needed. As the county seat, and a focus of the growing wool industry and railroad business, San Angelo did not require federal support or interference any longer. In 1889, the last contingents marched out of the fort and the federal presence that had protected and nurtured San Angelo in its infancy was ended.[22]

The contributions of the black soldiers were often overshadowed by the occasional clashes with townspeople. When Benjamin Grierson relinquished command of the district of the Pecos, he published a statement in the San Antonio paper that listed the accomplishments of the black troopers and their white officers. He noted the construction of barracks and quarters, the guarding of the mails and public property and the creation and maintenance of one thousand miles of wagon roads and three thousand miles of telegraph lines. In addition, the troops had scouted and surveyed over 135,710 miles of previously unexplored areas of Texas. He also cited the unrecognized efforts of the black troops who had pursued the Indians led by Victorio and wrote that even though they did not apprehend them, they harried them out of the United States and into the hands of the Mexican forces.[23]

It is difficult to discern if the problems the soldiers of Fort Concho faced at San Angelo were primarily of a racial origin or not. There was widespread resentment of the stationing of the black units in post-Reconstruction Texas. Newly freed slaves in uniform with the authority of the United States government behind them were almost certain to arouse animosity. There were, however, also clashes between white soldiers and civilians as Wedemeyer noted and the individual soldiers often bore the brunt of civilian resentment of the military presence they both demanded and resented. Therefore, although racial animosities were undoubtedly a factor, they should not be considered separately from the overall story of the occasionally tense relationship that existed between Fort Concho and the fledgling San Angelo.[24]

NOTES

[1.] William H. Leckie *The Buffalo Soldiers: A Narrative of the Negro Cavalry in the West* (Norman, Ok.: University of Oklahoma Press, 1967), 141; Medical History of Fort Concho, Texas, vol. 401, (copy at Fort Concho National Historic Landmark, herein after designated FCNHL), February 1870.

[2.] Medical History, vol. 401, February 1870; Leckie, *The Buffalo Soldiers*, 141-42.

[3.] Leckie, *The Buffalo Soldiers*, 149-52.

[4.] James Halm Ware, "San Angelo and San Antonio: A Comparative Study of the Military City in Texas, 1865-1898," (Master's thesis, Southwest Texas State University, 1973), 13, 47-48, 63, 114; Post Chaplain Records of the Adjutant General's Office A, Appointment, Commission and Personal Branch, Letters received from Chaplain Norman Badger, 1864-1883, microfilm, FCNHL, September 30, 1871.

[5.] Maj. William Wedemeyer, "Memoirs of William George Wedemeyer, USA, Major, Sixteenth Wisconsin Infantry: 1836-1902," typed reproduction of unpublished memoir, two volumes, FCNHL, vol. 1-20, 132, vol. 2, 99, 128-30.

[6.] Medical History, vol. 401, November 1871.

[7.] Ware, "San Angelo and San Antonio," 47-48, 56; Wedemeyer, "Memoirs," vol. 2, 99; Alice Grierson, letter to her son, Charles, December 28, 1875, xerox copy, FCNHL.

[8.] Post Chaplain Records, August 31, 1875; Medical History, November 1871; First Lt. John Bigelow, Jr., *Garrison Tangles in the Friendless Tenth*, Douglas C. McChristian, ed., (Bryan, Tex.: J.M. Carroll and Co., 1985), 1, 7, 21, 26.

[9.] Melton, "Trails by Nature," 89-90; Wedemeyer, "Memoirs," vol. 2, 100.

[10.] Green, "Ft. Concho: A Social History," 82-84; Post Chaplain Reports, February 29, 1876.

[11.] Leckie, *The Buffalo Soldier*, 163-64.

[12.] Wedemeyer "Memoirs," vol. 2, 100; San Antonio *Daily Express*, February 5, 1881, 1, February 16, 1881, 1.

[13.] Wedemeyer, "Memoirs," vol. 2, 100-101; Galveston *Weekly News*, February 3, 1881, 1, San Antonio *Daily Express*, February 11, 1881, 4.

[14.] Wedemeyer, "Memoirs," vol. 2, 102; San Antonio *Daily Express*, February 11, 1881, 4.

[15.] Wedemeyer, "Memoirs," vol. 2, 103-104; San Antonio *Daily Express*, February 11, 1881, 4; Galveston *Weekly News*, February 17, 1881.

[16.] Wedemeyer, "Memoirs," vol. 2, 106-107; Galveston *Weekly News*, February 17, 1881.

[17.] San Antonio *Daily Express*, Feb. 5, 1881, February 11, 1881, 4, February 16, 1881.

[18.] San Antonio *Daily Express*, February 5, 1881, 1, February 11, 1881, February 22, 1881, 1.

[19.] San Angelo *Standard*, May 3, 1924.

[20.] Leckie, *The Buffalo Soldiers*, 238; Medical History, vol. 407, n.p.; Wedemeyer, "Memoirs," vol. 2, 300; San Angelo *Standard*, September 15, 1888, 4.

[21.] Wedemeyer, "Memoirs," vol. 2, 299-300.

[22.] San Angelo *Standard*, May 3, 1924, January 26, 1978; Ware, "San Angelo and San Antonio," 59, 62.

[23.] *San Antonio Express Times*, February 20, 1881, 1.

[24.] J. Evetts Haley, "Racial Troubles on the Conchos," *The Black Military Experience in the American West*, John M. Carroll, ed., (New York: Liveright Publishing, 1971), 451-53. In his account, Haley blamed all the trouble between San Angelo and Fort Concho on the federal policy of placing black soldiers in Southern areas. His reporting of the uproar at San Angelo included errors such as the identification of the murdered soldier in Wedemeyer's company as black when all the soldiers in his 16th Infantry were white. Despite their admirable record, Haley did not believe that blacks could be qualified soldiers. In spite of these faults, his writing may reflect the resentment that many in early San Angelo felt towards the military and black soldiers in particular.

The Lost Treaty of the Black Seminoles

Eric Emmerson Strong

For over a hundred years, a small but curious crowd of historians and others has speculated about the existence of a rather unusual treaty. "The most remarkable thing about this particular treaty," says William Loren Katz, author *of Black Indians: A Hidden Heritage,* "is that a black Nation negotiated its entrance into the United States by formal treaty. It then arrived intact as a Nation, together with its reigning monarch, Chief John Horse."[1]

As farfetched as it might seem, there are those who will argue, and with great conviction, that a nation of black Indians, a people of both African and Indian ancestry, did indeed send their leaders to the Texas border in 1870 to hear the terms of a treaty being presented by an emissary of the U.S. government. Katz explains, "The U.S. Army had sent Captain Frank Perry to Mexico to negotiate an agreement with the black nation. In return for its young men serving as scouts for the army, families would be provided with food, necessities, and eventually some good farming land."[2]

The black Indian nation was never to be and the black Seminoles insisted that instead of getting a treaty from the government, all they ever got was "the treatment;"[3] just another snarl in the long string of broken promises made by the U.S. government with countless bands of Indian peoples. The government labeled them Seminole Negroes, and as the latter part of this name implies, a land grant treaty with people of African descent would have been an unprecedented action in the history of the United States government.

When the black Seminoles did ask the government to make good on its promise of land, questions were raised about who the Seminole Negroes really were. Were these Indians? That depends on whom you listen to. To the slave hunters, they were runaways. To those who sought to deny them their rights, they were no more than the Seminoles' slaves. To the anthropologists who studied them, they were maroons (both black and Indian). To the Mexicans who took them in, they were Muscogos, so named for the Muscogee Seminole dialect many of them spoke. Yet, there are those who contend that these so-called Seminole Negroes were actually more than merely the Seminoles' allies, more than Seminoles' kin. They argue that on occasion, they were the Seminoles' leaders.[4]

Whatever we choose to call them, their story is a tale of a tenacious people, engulfed in a desperate run for freedom and a quest for no less than a black Seminole nation. Their black chieftains, poised at the border, were "ready to talk treaty" with a United States government, which badly need their help.

Before addressing the issues concerning the validity or the whereabouts of the so-called lost treaty of the black Seminoles, it would be in order to summarize, in some detail, the chain of events that led to their peculiar position of strength at the bargaining table on that historic spring day in 1870.

Often in a mad dash toward freedom through the darkness of night, runaway slaves during the colonial era fled for the promised land in the province of Florida:

> Spain and England were enemies on land and sea, and each sought to undermine the stability of the other. Enticing slaves southward from the Carolinas and Georgia infuriated their British masters, so Spanish Florida held its doors open for runaways. However, few Blacks sought out the Spanish once they reached Florida. Instead, most seized the opportunity to live among the Seminole tribes or in all black towns along the river banks, . . .

Or so goes the gospel according Katz:[5]

> Out of the Florida wilderness these black pioneers cleared trees, built houses, and raised corn. Soon cattle, hogs, and horses roamed in the settlements. For generations black families prospered, children grew to adulthood, and livestock roamed near neat cabins. However, the men carried arms, a precaution against the constant threat of slaveholder invasions.[6]
>
> If they were allowed to remain free, the black Seminoles could become a threat to the whole slave system. But their former owners could not invade the Spanish colony to get them back, until the United States acquired Florida in 1821.[7]
>
> When the Congress declared in 1830 that all Indians were to be removed to a reservation west of the Mississippi, the Seminoles knowing their black relatives would go into bondage if they obeyed the law, refused to go. When the Army tried, first through negotiation and then by force, to separate the Indian Seminoles from their black friends and kinsmen, they succeeding only in igniting a bloody war.[8]

After eleven years of unsuccessful fighting, Commander Gen. William J. Worth concluded that the Army "couldn't whip" the rebels.[9] So the government informed the Seminoles that "if they would end their resistance, the blacks could go with them to Oklahoma."[10] Thus, traveling beside the Seminoles, traversing their own trail of tears, was a peculiar contingent of black men, women, and children.

Their confinement to the Territory during the slave era was anything but safe, for it meant black Seminoles were targeted by slave catchers, who often kidnapped black Seminole women and children and sold them to plantation owners in the southern states.[11]

Wild Cat, a Seminole chief and John Horse, a black Seminole sub-chief, led hundreds of Indians and blacks out of the Territory, away from clutches of slave hunters, through Texas, and across the border into Mexico during the fall of 1849.[12]

"In the summer of 1850, the Mexican authorities at Piedras Negras on the Rio Grande across from Eagle Pass were startled by the appearance of two hundred or so Seminole Indians and Negroes, whose leaders requested admission to Mexico as settlers."[13]

Head chief Wild Cat, sub chief John Horse, and two heavily armed warriors, met with Col. Juan Manual Maldanado, sub-inspector for the Colonias de Coahuila at San Fernado de Rosas, on July 12, 1850. The colonel provided tools, seeds, livestock, and ammunition to the immigrants. In return the newcomers were to guard the northern Mexico border against Texans and "los Indios barbaros" who raided Mexican settlements and retreated to the Texas side of the river.[14]

Hearing the pleas of the Seminoles for a homeland, President Antonio Lopez de Santa Anna awarded them "land never to be taken away." Wildcat and his band removed their people from La Navaja, to four *sitios* of granado mayor (pastureland measuring 6.6 miles square) at Alto, and other *sitios* in the *hacienda* of Naciemento in the Santa Rosa Mountains, northwest of Musquiz.[15]

For twenty years, seasoned black Seminole warriors patrolled the borderlands and their reputation as fighters and trackers grew far and wide. "As soldiers guarding the Rio Grande against rustlers and assorted desperadoes of every shade, the Black Seminoles rolled up an impressive record. In 20 battles they captured 432 horses and mules and killed 38 intruders. Not a single Seminole was killed or wounded. Some consider this a miracle."[16]

And so was the chain of events which found the black Seminole poised at the Texas-Mexico border, ready to sit down and "talk treaty" with a United States government, who badly needed their services as frontier scouts along the border.

The environment at the discussions was charged with great expectations. For the U.S. government, the negotiations represented a chance to at last protect Texas, and a chance to recruit a group of scouts to do the job who were both feared and respected. Their tenacity and incredible combat skills had been forged by victories in the Florida swamps and along the Texas border. For the black Seminoles, the treaty was everything. The prospect of a treaty meant a chance to gain a homeland in a United States, now free of slavery and embarked on a great era of reconstruction.

As expected, the U.S. emissary presented the black Seminoles with the Army's offer. Kenneth W. Porter, author of *The Negro on the American Frontier*, explains:

> Lt. Zenas R. Bliss of the 25th United States Cavalry, commanding at Fort Duncan, authorized Captain Frank W. Perry to visit Nacimiento and invite the Seminoles to return to the United States to serve as scouts. The Seminole understanding of the agreement finally arrived at between Captain Perry and John Kibbetts (a sub chief under John Horse), which the Negroes call 'de treaty' or sometimes 'the treatment' was that it provided that the government would pay the able-bodied young men's expenses for their provision for their families, and grants of land in return for their services as scouts.[17]

According to Kevin Mulroy, author of *Freedom on the Border: The Seminole Maroons in Florida, the Indian Territory, Coahuila, and Texas*, "John Kibbetts returned to Nacimiento to discuss the meeting with his people and to prepare for removal."[18]

"On July 4, 1870, the Kibbetts band arrived at Fort Duncan prepared to assume scout duties. The government provided the men with ammunition, rations, and carbines. The scouts provided their own horses. For the whites they were a strange, if not terrifying, sight. Most wore Indian clothing, and some sported war bonnets that included buffalo horns."[19]

The black Seminole scouts fought as if the treaty was written across their hearts. "In nine years under Bullis' command, the scouts compiled a prodigious record. In 26 engagements, 12 of them major, not a single scout was ever killed or wounded, even though they were sometimes outnumbered by the enemy 8 to 1."[20]

Though the scouts never numbered more than fifty, they won an unprecedented four coveted Medals of Honor during the height of the Indian wars. During this period, "the Seminole maroons played a major role in helping to clear West Texas of Indian bands hostile to white settlement of the area."[21]

Though the services rendered to the U.S. Army from 1870 to 1914, by the black Seminole Scouts was outstanding, "the land promised the recruits did not materialize. The War Department declared the Department out of land and the Indian Commissioner gave the matter a bureaucratic shrug."[22]

Many Americans would argue, so what? Broken treaties are as much a part of American history as are historical misstatements. To those countless Indian bands who all but disappeared, there was never any treaty more important than their own. There are those among Seminoles who remain convinced that a land grant treaty did exist.

The black Seminoles' belief in the government's failure to keep its agreement is evident in each appeal made by black Seminoles. Repeatedly, the black Seminoles sought help of government officials in obtaining the land they thought had been promised to them. At times, those who would appeal on black Seminoles' behalf, were themselves unconvinced that anything was owed to the black Seminoles.

Henry Breckenridge, Assistant Secretary of War to the Secretary of the Interior, was convinced that the government should help the black Seminoles, even it does not owe them anything. In a letter dated February 4, 1914, he writes:

> There is nothing of record to indicate that the government assumed any obligations for their maintenance (the black Seminoles), though they were allowed by the government to occupy lands and put up huts on the Fort Clark Military Reservation. They have been at Fort Clark for the last 30 or 40 years and have sort of a colony, so they naturally feel they have vested right in this land which they have been allowed to use and in the property they have acquired.

If the Interior Department could conveniently find a means of providing for these "Seminole Negro Indian Scouts, as indicated above, it would (to the War Department) be a very gratifying solution of this difficulty."[23]

The word from the Department of the Interior proved unfavorable for the black Seminoles. A.A. Jones, First Assistant Secretary, responded to Breckenridge's letter on March 27th of that same year. Like many others, Jones argued that the black Seminoles were not Indians. He echoed the government line in responding to the black Seminoles' pleas for help:

> If any rights as Indians still existed in these people it would come by virtue of their Seminole blood. By section 2 of the Act of April 26, 1907 (34 Stats. L., 137), the rolls of the Seminole tribe were closed as of March 4, 1907, since which date the Secretary of the Interior has no power to add any names thereto. Having no other Indian blood in their veins they would not be entitled, under existing laws, to either land or money with any of the Indian tribes of the United States. It is not seen, there, how this Department is in a position to extend any relief to the person referred to in your communications.[24]

In an effort to mount an effective argument, the black Seminole compiled a list of the scouts indicating each scout's nationality. They hoped this list would convince the Secretary of the Interior that the Seminoles did indeed share Seminole ancestry. Of the twenty scouts listed on the petition, not one of the scouts listed his nationality as pure "Negro." The following list accompanied the February 12, 1914, letter from Henry Breckenridge, Assistant Secretary of War and mailed to A.A. Jones, First Assistant Secretary of the Interior:

Name	Nationality as Stated by Scout himself
1. Charles Daniels	Seminole and Creek
2. Fay July	Seminole
3. Caesar Daniels	Seminole and Cherokee
4. John Daniels	Seminole and Creek
5. Thomas Daniels	Seminole
6. Curley Jefferson	Seminole and Mexican
7. John Jefferson	Seminole
8. Billy July	Seminole and Creek
9. Charles J. July	Seminole and Negro
10. George Kibbits	Seminole and Creek
11. Ignacio Perryman	Seminole and Mexican
12. Joseph Phillips	Seminole and Creek
13. Joe Remo	Seminole and Choctaw
14. Antonio Sanchez	Mexican
15. John Shields	Seminole
16. Carolino Warrior	Seminole and Negro
17. Sam Washington	Seminole
18. Billy Wilson	Seminole
19. Isaac Wilson	Seminole and Creek
20. William Wilson	Seminole and Creek[25]

On August 14, 1914, Senator Morris Sheppard, Chairman of the Committee for Expenditure on Agriculture, entered the effort to help the black Seminoles obtain the illusive land grant. Sheppard wrote to Cato Sells, Commissioner of Indian Affairs:

> Please note the enclosed letter and clipping referring to the Seminole Indians. I do not know anything about the

merits of this proposition but if the facts set forth in the letter and clipping are true, it certainly seems that these Indians should have considerate treatment.

Kindly give the matter attention and let me know what you think about it.[26]

On September 4, 1914, Sells responded to Senator Sheppard's letter, admitting to some, but denying most of the Seminoles Indian ancestry, he wrote: "Our records indicate that these people have very little Indian blood and they are practically all Negroes."[27]

The extent of Indian blood among the black Seminole scouts is still debated. However, some validity may be attributed to their claim when one considers that "the number of Afro Americans with an Indian ancestor was once estimated at about one third of the total."[28]

Doug Sivad, author of *Black Seminole Indians of Texas* makes the point about black Seminole chief John Horse:

> The black factions (maroons and estelusti) were valuable to the Indian Seminoles, and, although most blacks preferred to marry blacks and live in their own towns, miscegenation continued between Africans and Indians. Juan Cavallo (John Horse) was born to an Indian father and a black Indian mother, c. 1810. The Indians considered him as an "Indyen" but because of his ginger colored skin, whites classified him as black. . . .[29]

Katz argues that one symbol of the unity of the two races is that many believe the second Seminole War of 1835 began when Seminole Chief Osceola's black wife was kidnapped by U.S. troops.[30]

There were those who remained convinced that the blacks were indeed Seminoles and endeavored to persuade others that the black Seminoles' service had earned them more than lip service. Apparently undaunted by his lack of success to obtain a homeland for the black Seminoles, Breckenridge continued lobbying on behalf of the black Seminoles. He responded to the Department of the Interior's failure to recognize the black Seminoles as Indians, by offering land to the Department of the Interior so that it might be awarded as a homeland for the black Seminoles. On May 14, 1914, Breckenridge responded to Jones' letter: "Should the reservation of Fort Clark, which consists of 3,963 acres, be turned over to the Department of the Interior, would it be practicable to allot lands to these people on the reservation? About 225 acres of reservation land are now under cultivation by the people."[31]

Many believe 225 acres is the land promised by treaty to the black Seminoles, including Beth Bradley, a retired librarian from Del Rio. Ms. Bradley said that in 1952, she actually saw a copy of the treaty. She said she ordered it from Washington, D.C., as per the request of a patron of the library. She said the patron, an elderly black man, came back two years later saying he had lost the copy of the treaty. She said she tried to retrieve the copy from government document sources again, but was unsuccessful.[32]

Most people who study the Seminoles remain doubtful of the existence of a black Seminole treaty. However, the following letter suggests what may have happened to the treaty. The letter, sent August 18, 1932, from Congressman J.H. Brooks, Assistant Secretary of Indian Affairs to the Commissioner of Indian Affairs, makes a case for reparations:

> We are in receipt of a communication regarding the claim of Mrs. Nellie Best, widow of William Best, deceased Spanish War veteran, based upon a treaty under which payments were made to the Seminole Indians in lieu of land and rations. This letter reads as follows:
>
> The facts are as follows: about 1870, Major Perry of the 9th U.S. Cavalry persuaded Pompey Factor, a Seminole Indian, to induce the Seminoles to return to the United States and join the Indian Scouts. Later Major Perry went to Santa Rosa, Mexico, where he talked with Seminole Chief John Kibbetts and persuaded him to bring his people back to the United States. A treaty was signed and agreement made whereby the Seminoles' expenses were paid and many men joined the Texas Scouts. In 1870,

another agreement was made whereby the government agreed to furnish the Seminoles with provisions of land together with horses, plows, farming equipment, etc. Under these treaties and agreements the Seminoles returned to the United States in 1870 and stayed on the reservation set aside for them until 1913, at which time the Seminoles were disbanded and Col. Shelby of the 13th Cavalry visited the reservation and asked to be shown the treaty papers. For some reason, the treaty had been left at Santa Rosa, Mexico, and John Shields, a First Sergeant, was sent to bring the treaty back to the United States. At that time a Mexican revolution was in progress and before the treaty could be obtained, the courthouse at Santa Rosa was destroyed and the records lost. The Seminoles lived on the reservation for 52 years and in 1917 Alexander Powell was sent from Washington by President Wilson to enroll the Seminoles. J. Blackman, his wife and daughter enrolled the names and went to Mexico to get the names of the Seminoles who did not come to the United States. Mr. Blackman was a cattleman of Brakettville [sic], Texas, and as bondsmen required each Seminole to deposit $5.00. Those who did not pay the $5.00 received a loan from him and he posted a bond of $2500.00. We are informed that he is still alive and willing to furnish any information necessary to collaborate this statement. In 1917, Mrs. Best was sent for in regard to this matter and went to Fort Clark, Texas to make her proof. While there Major Powell told all the people that they were to receive $2,000.00 each under the treaty and agreement rights in lieu of land and rations. We would greatly appreciate your comment in this connection in a letter which we might quote our correspondent.[33]

In replying to Brooks letter, Acting Commissioner Garber, responded, again maintaining the government line in regards to the black Seminoles:

These scout left the Seminole Indian Nation in Oklahoma. If they ever had rights, they were given prior to the time the rolls of these Indians were closed in 1907, under the Act of April 26th, 1906 (34 Stat. L., 137). They therefore have no treaty rights as Seminole Indians or freedmen.

It appears also from our record that these scouts possessed very little, if any, Indian blood.[34]

The claim that the black Seminoles had little or no Indian blood is particularly ironic when viewed in light of the fact the unit's official name, "Seminole Negro Indian Scouts," was coined out of necessity. "They had to be classified as Indians to be placed on the payroll as scouts," notes Charles Downing a Seminole history buff. "The 1866 congress act that authorized establishing black regiments included a provision for hiring Indians, but not blacks, as scouts."[35] It would appear that the black Seminoles were classified and reclassified as a matter of government convenience.

And what of the lost treaty? Was it, too, merely a document of temporary convenience meant to lure black Seminoles into service as scouts? What of the claim made by Nellie Best in 1932? Was the treaty destroyed during the Mexican revolution along with the courthouse at Santa Rosa?[36] Or, is it somewhere in a dusty attic in Del Rio among the belongings of the library patron whom Bess Bradley claimed received a copy in 1952?[37] Or did it burn in 1879 along with John Kibbetts' house, as Seminole John Jefferson theorized during a 1950 interview with Kenneth Porter?[38] Or was a copy found in Santa Rosa and sent to Mexico City to be copied between 1935 and 1940, as was reported to Porter by sources in Brackettville during his 1941 interviews?[39] Or did Kibbetts negotiate a treaty for a land grant? Perhaps it is no more than wishful speculation.

Donald Swanson, Curator of the Fort Clark Historical Association, contends that, "There was no treaty. Perry did not have any authority to even sign a treaty."[40]

Kevin Mulroy, doubts that a treaty was ever signed. "If it was an agreement, it was probably a verbal agreement."[41]

When asked if he thought there was ever a treaty, Tom Senter, an expert on the black Seminoles, replied, "I wouldn't put money on it."[42]

When she was asked about the lost treaty, Black Seminole tribal historian and community matriarch, Charles Emily Wilson of Brackettville, explained, "I really don't think there was a treaty. Because if there was, that treaty would have probably turned up by now. It's been too many people looking for it."[43]

Dub Warrior, president of the Black Seminole Scouts Association, said, "I don't know. Could've been, and then again, maybe not."[44]

In 1946, John Jefferson offered a $500 reward for the recovery of the lost treaty of the black Seminoles.[45] Was there ever a lost treaty or was it a part of the myth of the American western frontier? The answer to that question could not be found in this report. Its recovery, if it does exist, will represent an important milestone in the history of the American West—a milestone which will build new hope and self-esteem to those who share the legacy of the black Seminole Indians.

NOTES

[1] William Loren Katz, *Black Indians: A Hidden Heritage* (Simon Pulse, 1997), 76.

[2] Ibid., 76-77.

[3] Kenneth Wiggins Porter, *The Negro on the American Frontier* (Ayer Co. Pub., 1971), 475.

[4] Ibid., 277.

[5] Willam Loren Katz, *Black People Who Made the Old West* (Thomas Y. Crowell, 1977), 18.

[6] Ibid., 19.

[7] Bryan Wooley, "Freedom Fighters," *Dallas Life Magazine*, February 2, 1992, p. 8.

[8] Ibid., pp. 8-9.

[9] Ibid., p. 9.

[10] Ibid.

[11] Katz, *Black People Who Made the Old West*, 144.

[12] Doug Sivad, *The Black Seminole Indians of Texas* (Sivad Group, 1986), 12.

[13] Kenneth W. Porter, "The Seminole in Mexico," *The National Hispanic American Review*, February 1951, p. 1.

[14] Sivad, *The Black Seminole Indians of Texas*, 13-14.

15. Ibid., 20-21.

16. Katz, *Black People Who Made the Old West*, 144.

17. Porter, *The Negro on the American Frontier*, 475.

18. Kevin Mulroy, *Freedom on the Border: The Seminole Maroons in Florida, the Indian Territory, Coahuila, and Texas* (Lubbock, Tex.: Texas Tech University Press, 2003), 112.

19. Katz, *Black People Who Made the Old West*, 144.

20. Keith Wheeler, *The Old West: The Scouts* (New York: Time Life Books, 1978), 116.

21. Mulroy, *Freedom on the Border*, 117.

22. Wheeler, *The Scouts*, 6.

23. Henry Breckenridge, Assistant Secretary of War, to the Secretary of the Interior, February 4, 1914.

24. First Assistant Secretary, A.A. Jones to Breckenridge, Assistant Secretary of War, March 27, 1914.

25. Henry Breckenridge, Assistant Secretary of War to A.A. Jones, First Assistant Secretary of the Interior, February 12, 1914.

26. Senator Morris Sheppard, Chairman of the Committee for Expenditure on Agriculture, to Cato Sells, Commissioner of Indian Affairs, August 14, 1914.

27. Cato Sells, Commissioner of Indian Affairs, to Senator Morris Sheppard, Chairman of the Committee for Expenditure on Agriculture, September 4, 1914.

28. Katz, *Black Indians*, 3.

29. Sivad, *The Black Seminole Indians*, 6.

30. Katz, *Black Indians*, 3.

31. Henry Breckenridge, Assistant Secretary of War to A.A. Jones, First Assistant Secretary of the Interior, May 14, 1914.

32. Bess Bradley, Retired Librarian, personal interview, February 20, 1996.

33. Congressman J.H. Brooks, Assistant Secretary of Indian Affairs, to the Commissioner of Indian Affairs, August 4, 1932.

34. Acting Commissioner Garber, Commissioner of Indian Affairs to Congressman J.H. Brooks, Assistant Secretary of Indian Affairs, August 18, 1932.

35. Kevin C. Swisher, "Frontier Heroes," *Texas Highways*, July 1992, p. 49.

36. Congressman J.H. Brooks, Assistant Secretary of Indian Affairs, to the Commissioner of Indian Affairs.

37. Bess Bradley, retired Librarian, personal interview, February 20, 1996.

38. John Jefferson, black Seminole, interview with Kenneth Porter, August 20, 1950.

39. Unnamed sources among the black Seminoles of Brackettville, Texas, sources, personal interviews with Kenneth W. Porter, 1941.

40. Donald Swanson, President of the Brackettville Historical Society, personal interview, April 15, 1996.

41. Kevin Mulroy, historian, personal interview, February 27, 1996.

42. Tom Senter, historian, personal interview, February 27, 1996.

43. Charles Emily Wilson, tribal historian, personal interview, February 27, 1996.

44. Willie Warrior, president Black Seminole Scouts Association, personal interview, February 27, 1996.

45. John Jefferson, black Seminole, letter to Kenneth W. Porter, historian, July 12, 1946.

Abilene's Minority Population and the 1900 Census

Karen Turner

Every decade community leaders protest that the United States Census Bureau has undercounted their city. Along with this cry is its corollary: the minorities in the town are not accurately enumerated. Abilene's *Twelfth Census* was another verse to this chronic undercount complaint for the reported population of 3,411 residents was unacceptable.

Abilene's boosters worried about a possible undercount even as the two enumerators completed their survey in June of 1900. The *Abilene Reporter* quoted favorably the *El Paso Times*' claim that "the census will be a farce unless more time is allowed." Only a week after the Abilene's census workers, Nannie Mae Sellers and C. Charles Malone, completed their work, the newspaper argued that, for so much territory, not enough time was allowed, resulting in an undercount. In October, the newspaper voiced criticism of the whole census finding and suggested the school census was much more accurate, concluding that Abilene must have nearly 5,000 people.[2] Further evidence came from the Sanborn Insurance map of Abilene in 1902, which gave the population as 5,200, much more than the 3,411 citizens that the census workers reported.

George Anderson, Abilene's newspaper manager, angrily editorialized, "the government census had never done the town justice."[3] He judged the work of Abilene's enumerators unsatisfactory and claimed that he could find and name over 1,000 overlooked inhabitants. To make good on that claim, he and his associate, John L. Stephenson, produced their own count, publishing the results in a 1905 city directory. Stephenson listed only the names of the white citizens and estimated that total to be more than 5,000, a much larger count than the 3,218 white citizens Malone and Sellers found five years previously. Either the *Twelfth Census* erred in over-looking significant numbers of citizens or Abilene experienced a 68 per cent population growth in half a decade.

Although the city had doubtless benefited from immigration between 1900 and 1905, strong evidence suggested that Sellers and Malone simply missed counting many of their fellow inhabitants. They were even less diligent in their count of minority citizens. The Anderson-Stephenson directory found 368 blacks and 149 Hispanics, more than double the 1900 census figures for blacks (171) and over seven times the number for Hispanics (19).

The minorities lived in no special area in Abilene and their numbers formed but a small percentage of the town's population. The census recorded 3,411 citizens, with 5.66 per cent of this total classed as minorities. The south side had 1,928 whites, 19 Hispanics, 65 blacks and 3 Chinese, for a total of 2,015 or 59.07 per cent of the total population. The north side recorded 1,290 whites and 106 black and no Hispanics or Orientals for a total of 1,396 or 40.92 per cent of the total population.[4] The white population was 94.89 per cent of the town's total, while in the nation as a whole the percentage was smaller, 87.9 per cent. This larger than average white population seems unremarkable, for Abilene was not found-

99

ed until sixteen years after the Civil War. There were no freed slaves or the lure of plentiful jobs to draw additional blacks to the community. Black citizens constituted only 5 per cent of the population.

Few blacks lived in the city when Will Henderson moved to Abilene in 1904. The first black man to serve on a jury and the first to cast an absentee ballot in the Democratic primary, he recalled that blacks "were as scarce as hen's teeth."[6] Henderson estimated the black population to be 250-300 in 1904, and by 1905 John Stephenson counted 368 blacks, although he did not include their names in his 1905 directory. Stephenson wrote, "We deem it unnecessary to give the names of the Negroes and Mexicans in this work but have counted them. This was 115 per cent increase from the census count of 1900. Either many blacks moved to Abilene from 1900 to 1905, or the enumerators and/or Stephenson miscounted.

In 1901 Will Stith did record black citizens using the designation "col." meaning colored. His directory listed 212 black citizens, one-fourth more than the census of the previous year.[8] Also the black community, including most of the unskilled workers and a prostitute, was in Seller's district. One can imagine that the young white teenager moved quickly and did not return to the neighborhood for missed residents.

Will Stith, another real estate man, published *A Census and Directory of the City of Abilene 1901* and included the names of black citizens.[9] The census, a map and a 1901 directory combined locate each of the twenty-four residences of blacks listed by Abilene's census takers.

These sources indicate that sixty-five blacks lived on the south side of town. Of these, nine were servants living in the homes of their employers. Dr. Lawrence W. Hollis, Sr., had more black servants than anyone in town, the four members of the Pearce family.[10] Other employers were physicians, attorneys, and a grain dealer. The fifty-six blacks, living in their own thirteen separate dwellings, recorded mainly unskilled occupations such as cook, washer, seamstress, porter, and laborer. Miss Ada Hillsman, an eighteen year old teacher, and Berry Smith, a fifty-two year old preacher from Virginia, were the only two with skilled occupations.[11] Most blacks lived on Willow Street with sixteen black residents, followed by Cherry Street with fourteen and Locust with eleven. Eleven of the dwellings clustered between South Fifth and Second.

The north side had more blacks, 106. Twenty-six were servants and lived with the families that employed them, those of bankers, lawyers, druggists, newspapermen, and grocers. Two blacks lived and worked as a waiter and porter in the Windsor Hotel.[12] Seventy-eight blacks lived in thirteen separate dwellings and were unskilled laborers, excepting two ministers. Most rented their homes, and twenty-eight lived on Plum Street, eleven on Ash, ten on Hickory and nine on Mesquite. Ash Street was unique for it was the only one in town in which every resident was black.[13]

Will Henderson recalled that by 1904 the blacks were in a "cluster in an area from North First to North Sixth streets, between Mesquite and Ash Streets, north of the Texas and Pacific Railway. There were a few houses south of the T&P railroad on Willow, China, and Cherry Streets."[14] The census authenticates Henderson's memory.

One black wash woman, Millie McCline, lived in Abilene in 1900. She gave no date to the enumerator for her birth on a large plantation in Lynnville, Tennessee, during the 1850's. "Aunt Millie" came to Abilene with the J.M. Wagstaff family, and later cared for the children of the Minter and Sayles families.[15] At the time of the 1900 census, this divorced mother of twelve lived on Cypress Street with five of her seven living children.[16]

Residing in the northwest edge of town on Beech Street was Edmond Dortch.[17] He operated Abilene's first barbershop, located on North Fifth and Pine.[18] Dortch was one of the few skilled workers among the minority population. On the south side Doke Johns lived on Willow Street with his wife Annie and two boarders, a train porter and a teacher.[19] Johns, one of the few Willow

Street residents in a minor professional occupation, clerked for about fifty years in Ed Hughes' Hardware Store.[20]

In contrast, Taylor Avant of Cherry Street practiced a host of occupations. In addition to selling Hokey-Pokey ice cream, he ran a cafe, a skating rink, and a catering service as well.[21] Born in North Carolina before emancipation, in 1900 he lived with his wife Lucy, a daughter and four step-children on Cherry Street.[22]

In 1900 blacks owning their own homes resided in two areas: in the southeast near the earliest school and church for blacks and in the northeast among unskilled laborers along Plum and Ash streets. By 1901, there was a migration of blacks to the northeast; the two families that lived on Locust Street in 1900 had moved to Cottonwood in the northeast part of town. Millie McCline also moved to the northeast on Ash Street between North Second and Third. The two residents further to the west, Bushy Kyle and Lawrence McQueen, were not listed in the 1901 directory at all; perhaps they had moved from the city.[23] The school and church followed. Until 1902 the Abilene Colored School met in Mount Zion Baptist Church located on the southwest corner of Cherry and South Fourth. By 1907 the Colored Ward School was relocated to North Seventh between Magnolia and Ash, and three other churches for blacks were built.[24] This was the cluster Will Henderson recalled. The reason for this migration to the beginnings of a segregated neighborhood in the northeast after 1900 were not apparent. Perhaps as the black population increased, the opportunities for fellowship, school and church located there made it a more desirable area.

Little was written concerning the blacks except for successful businessmen and beloved servants. The newspaper rarely printed a story about Abilene's black citizens. On June 8, 1900, there was an article on a "colored man" named Bush who grew crops particularly well despite the rain of the previous week.[25] The article seemed to have an underlying message that Bush was involved in a perfectly accepted role, working hard and diligently cultivating crops. Another story concerned the election of J.A.S. Harvey as teacher for the "colored school;"[26] neither Bush or Harvey, however, were listed in the 1900 census.

Although black citizens lived and worked in Abilene, the census was one of the few documents that recorded their lives. Evidently the census undercounted this minority; judging from the attitude in Stephenson's 1905 directory, this was the accepted view, an unrecorded community. But if the blacks were small in numbers, other minorities in 1900 were even smaller.

Hispanics were a tiny percentage (.55 per cent) of Abilene's population in 1900. Eighteen were day laborers living in three adjacent dwellings on Willow Street in southeast Abilene.[27] A tailor, P.L. Carpio, lived alone on Chestnut.[28] Possibly the census missed many Hispanics, since Stephenson's 1905 directory claimed "149 Mexicans," although he declined, as he did with blacks, to list their names in his directory.[29]

Willow Street was an ethnic mix in 1900. To the far south lived whites, working mainly as day laborers. Then between South Fourth and South Third stood four dwellings of blacks, including those of Doke Johns. Then came residences of the Hispanics, all day laborers. The street ended at South First with the home of a white widow, Mrs. Rugar, whose son and another white laborer lived with her.

Three Chinese men lived in Abilene in one dwelling, a house rented by W. Sing, S. Guo and Wong Lock were laundrymen as was Mr. Sing; Guo was born in California, the other two in China.[30] Naomi Kincaid wrote of two Chinese laundries in the late 1880's owned by John Sing.[31] No John Sing appeared in the 1900 census but W. Sing may well have been this entrepreneur. Abilenians recalled very white clothes and very stiff collars from the Sing laundry, and Julia Belle Williams Beene remembered that the Asian workers wore white coats and pants and braided their long hair in two long "twigs." When a modern steam laundry opened, the Chinese laundry closed and the men left Abilene.[32]

Blacks, Hispanics and Orientals comprised Abilene's minority community. The blacks attended a separate school and churches located in their own neighborhood. The *Twelfth Census* failed to locate some of their members, for the town's social and economic dynamics made them a separate community, perhaps partially invisible to the white enumerators.

NOTES

1. *The Abilene Reporter*, June 22, 1900, p. 4, col. 1.

2. *The Abilene Reporter*, October 26, 1900, p. 6, col. 1.

3. "Abilene Before 1905," *West Texas Genealogical Society Bulletin* 13 (1971), p. 17.

4. U.S. Department of Commerce, *Twenty Censuses: Population and Housing Questions, 1790-1980* (Washington D.C.: Government Printing Office, 1979), p. 33. The census used only three codes for color or race: a "B" for black, a "Ch" for Chinese, and a "W" for white and all others. Although the census did not separate the Hispanic population, those with Mexico as the place of birth and obvious Spanish surnames were identified as Hispanics in this study.

5. Otto Johnson, ed., *1988 Information Please Almanac* (Boston: Houghton Mifflin Company, 1988), 769.

6. "Making a Living," *Abilene Remembered: Our Centennial Treasury Book, 1881-1981* (Abilene: *Abilene Reporter News*, 1981), 33.

7. John Stephenson, *Abilene City Directory* (Abilene: Stephenson, 1905), 20.

8. Will Stith, *A Census and Directory of the City of Abilene 1901* (Abilene: Will Stith and Company, 1901), n.p.

9. Stith, *Census*, n.p.

10. United States Department of Commerce, Bureau of the Census, *Twelfth Census of the United States, 1900*, Taylor County, Texas, Enumeration District 149, p. 22. Hereinafter the census will be cited by enumeration districts (149 Malone's district on the south and 150 Sellers' district on the north) and page.

11. *Twelfth Census*, 149, p. 2, 3.

12. *Twelfth Census*, 150, p.11.

13. *Twelfth Census*, 150, p. 15.

14. "Making a Living," 33.

15. Jack North, *Pioneers of the Abilene Area* (Abilene: Jack North, 1978), 36.

16. *Twelfth Census*, 150, p.13.

17. *Twelfth Census*, 150, p. 7.

18. Jewell Pritchett, *The Black Community in Abilene* (Abilene: Pritchett Publications, 1984), 12.

19. *Twelfth Census*, 149, p. 3.

20. "Making a Living," 33.

21. Ibid.

22. *Twelfth Census*, 149, p. 3.

23. *Twelfth Census*, 149, p. 24; *Twelfth Census*, 150, p. 7; Stith, *Census and Directory*, 77.

[24] Juanita Zachary, *Abilene: The Key City* (Northridge, Calif.: Windsor Publications, 1986), 38.

[25] *Abilene Reporter*, June 8, 1900, p. 5.

[26] *Abilene Reporter*, May 4, 1900, p. 7, col. 6.

[27] *Twelfth Census*, 149, p. 3.

[28] *Twelfth Census*, 149, p. 10.

[29] Stephenson, *Abilene Directory*, 20.

[30] *Twelfth Census*, 149, p. 12.

[31] Naomi Hatten Kincaid, "The *Abilene Reporter News* and Its Contribution to the Building of the Abilene Country" (Masters thesis, Hardin-Simmons University, 1945), 112.

[32] Julia Belle Williams Beene, "My Story While I Lived in Abilene, Texas," *West Texas Geneological Society Bulletin* 22 (1980), p. 17.

Black Lubbock

Robert L. Foster and Alwyn Barr

The first black people to see the Lubbock area on the plains of West Texas came as soldiers with the Spanish expedition of Francisco Coronado, which explored what is today the Southwestern United States in 1540-1541. The region remained unsettled, by anyone other than Indians, until the late nineteenth century after the American Civil War had emancipated the black slaves of the South. As settlers appeared on the Great Plains of the United States in the 1870s, black frontiersmen filled two important roles in the developing new society—soldiers and ranch hands. All four black regiments of the United States Army, the 9th and 10th Cavalry and the 24th and 25th Infantry, served on the frontier and crossed the West Texas plains area. The expeditions of these black troopers helped control raids by Indians, who called them "Buffalo Soldiers," and speeded settlement by collecting information on the location of water and fuel. Blacks worked as cooks, cowboys and horse wranglers for several of the ranchers on the plains. A wagon driver for the IOA Ranch in Lubbock County during the 1880s became the first black man to live near the site of the future city. The 1890 United States Census listed two black men in Lubbock County, both probably with the IOA Ranch, but they had disappeared along with the ranch by 1900, as white farmers began to settle the area and founded the town of Lubbock.[1]

These new white land owners first developed small family farms with little need for additional workers. Many white settlers opposed any black residents in the small community and the Lubbock *Avalanche* during January 1910, expressed their views in strong terms. "This is white man's country and it should not be polluted by a lot of worthless 'niggers.'" Thus it is not surprising that the census of 1910 indicated only five blacks in Lubbock, with an increase to just sixteen by 1917. Will Sedberry, a cook in the Merrill Hotel in 1911, left because of such hostility, but returned in 1922. Yet Earl Johnson and Calvin Quigley became two of the first permanent settlers in the town by buying land during this period. Economic pressure turned the tide against efforts to exclude all blacks.[2]

Cotton became an increasingly profitable crop in the early twentieth century, especially after it was possible to ship the crop out by railroad beginning in 1909. As farms grew in size farmers tried to meet their labor needs by bringing in black and Mexican-American migrant workers from East and South Texas beginning in 1910. In 1919 farmers began to raise far more cotton than in the past, which led to a rapid increase in black population as dozens of farm workers came in to help with the crops. By 1920 Lubbock County counted 152 blacks. Although most of them lived on farms, sixty-three had settled in the town of Lubbock, being 1.6 per cent of its 4,051 people. Their move, generally from East and Central Texas, had been caused by some of the same factors which led thousands of black people to leave the South and settle in northern cities during this same period. Low wages and problems with the boll weevil on cotton farms were primary factors, although the hope of escaping prejudice and lynchings also influenced black people to move.[3]

Early black settlers in Lubbock often lived in servants quarters near the homes of their employers throughout the small town. Opposition by some whites led to residential segregation, the writing of a city ordinance in 1923 that restricted blacks to a section of southeastern Lubbock. Apparently the city commission never adopted the ordinance, but most whites seem to have supported the concept by refusing to sell or rent land and houses to blacks outside that area. Residential segregation by law and by custom reflected national patterns of the period, despite a Supreme Court decision in 1917 against legal separation of housing.[4]

Selection of southeast Lubbock as the black section resulted because some blacks already had bought small lots and begun to set up tents, dugouts and later narrow frame houses in the blocks between Avenues A and C and 16th and 19th Streets, which became known as the "flats." In the mid-1920s blacks began to expand their residential area by moving farther southeast, the only direction open to them, into the Wheelock Second Addition east of Avenue A and south of 19th Street. In both black sections water came from wells and all toilets were outside during the 1920s and 1930s. Expansion resulted from continued growth of the black community, which counted 1,100 persons in 1930, 5.4 per cent of Lubbock's 20,520 people. By 1940 the black population had increased to 2,229, or 7 per cent of the town's 31,853 residents.[5]

Blacks in Lubbock faced other forms of discrimination in addition to segregated housing. Theaters offered only separate balcony seats, while restaurants served blacks in rooms behind their kitchens. The first bus company did not have to pick up blacks, and could carry them only in a separate bus or section of a bus. Local newspaper coverage emphasized negative stereotypes of blacks as lazy or engaged in crime and vice such as gambling, bootlegging, and prostitution, though some whites probably encouraged such activities. The Ku Klux Klan, which revived throughout the nation in the 1920s to promote a rather narrow view of morality as well as anti-immigrant and anti-black views, existed in Lubbock and tried to intimidate its black citizens on at least one occasion. To these forms of prejudice black leaders in Lubbock replied at times with assurances that they too opposed vice and crime, and would be happy to support civic projects if offered an opportunity.[6]

Within such a segregated society blacks came into contact with whites most often as employees. Large numbers of black women and some men worked as domestic servants in white homes at wages of $5 to $7 a week. Most other blacks labored on farms near town, or for hotels, restaurants, railroads, and local stores at generally low wages. A few black businesses also developed to serve the separate community. Guy Cefres opened the first cafe and pool hall, followed by the Sedberry's in the early 1920s. Jake White and Waymon Henry operated the first barber shop. By 1935 the black section also included a hotel, a cleaning shop, a laundry, a funeral home, a tailor, a taxi company, and two grocers. Yet low wages and limited credit made it impossible for most blacks to consider beginning a business of their own.[7]

A limited number of black law officers served during the 1920s and 1930s, but by the 1930s they could not arrest whites. Some had reputations as too tough on other blacks and lost their jobs because they used their pistols too freely. In 1932 Dr. Joel P. Oliver arrived to become Lubbock's first black doctor, who treated black and white patients. The first black dentist, Dr. C.H. Lyons, moved to town the following year. When Oliver left after his marriage to a white woman in New Mexico, he was replaced in 1939 by Dr. J.A. Chatman who opened the first black hospital in 1945.[8]

Blacks in Lubbock faced increased unemployment and wage cuts in the 1930s as a result of the nation-wide economic depression. Black workers in low paying jobs suddenly met greater competition from whites who had lost better positions. The town and federal governments provided relief and jobs for the unemployed. Local blacks received from 1 to 8 per cent of the aid in different programs. Black churches, individually at first and later through an organized Colored Relief Association, provided free meals for the unemployed. In comparison to larger, more industrialized cities, however, the depression unemployment level remained lower and the resulting hardships less severe for blacks in Lubbock.[9]

Black social life existed on a separate basis in the "flats" on weekends, as in most black communities during the 1920s. It centered around Bob Johnson's dance hall, some gambling at Cefres's cafe, bootleg liquor, and trips to the more wide open railroad town of Slaton, fifteen miles southeast. A black house of prostitution existed in Lubbock in the 1920s but was soon forced to close. Bob and Earl Johnson organized a baseball team in the 1920s called the Black Rubbers, which played both black and white teams. Booker T. Washington Park provided a place for outdoor recreation beginning in 1929, though it was poorly landscaped. In the 1930s social activities expanded to include style shows, musicals, and Christmas parties, often held in churches. Annual celebrations of emancipation on June 19, popularly called "Juneteenth," provided the major event of each year with a picnic, a dance, speeches, and games.[10]

More permanent forms of social organization developed with the growth of black population, following patterns well established during the nineteenth century. A Masonic lodge was established in 1920, followed by the Knights of Pythias, and the Eastern Star about 1924. An Odd Fellows chapter existed briefly but failed. These groups held regular meetings and occasional parades and barbeques. In 1938 the Dunbar Parent-Teachers Association and another group of black citizens created two Boy Scout troops. Troop 18 had Charles Sedberry as scoutmaster, while Troop 19, sponsored by the PTA, was led by Perry Jackson. During World War II, the American Legion organized Booker T. Washington Post 808 for black veterans in Lubbock. New fraternal groups continued to organize in the 1960s, such as the Elks and Alpha Phi Alpha.[11]

Religious life for black people also happened within the separate community of East Lubbock. Again this followed national patterns developed in the nineteenth century, as blacks sought to avoid discrimination and to attain positions of leadership by founding their own churches and denominations. Because of social segregation, black churches also became the focus of many activities in addition to worship services. In 1917 Ida Stafford began to hold Sunday School classes in her home, which developed into Mt. Gilead Baptist Church. Carter Chapel Christian Methodist Episcopal Church organized in a similar way during 1920, as did Bethel African Methodist Episcopal Church in 1921. In 1925 Messiah Presbyterian Church and Mosley Chapel, which became Mt. Vernon Methodist Episcopal Church, were established, followed in 1928 by the Church of God in Christ and other Baptist congregations. Some met outdoors in good weather until buildings could be constructed. The number of black churches continued to grow as the population increased, and by the 1970s reached twenty or more.[12]

Traveling ministers came on a part-time basis in the early years. Limited funds forced the Mt. Gilead congregation to appeal for white aid in constructing the first black church, a small two-room building in 1918. Yet black people relied primarily upon their own efforts to sustain their churches. William Sedberry, for example, raised money for five years to pay for the first Presbyterian building. Despite the variety of denominations, black churches held cooperative activities such as revivals, dramatic performances, and social gatherings. Finally, churches also provided early locations for education in the black community.[13]

During World War I, Lubbock briefly had integrated education as a few black pupils attended a downtown elementary school. In 1920 the school board somewhat reluctantly hired its first black teacher, Sadie Taylor, who held separate classes in servants' quarters at an annual salary of about three-fourths the amount paid white teachers. A Mrs. Butler taught black pupils the following school year in Mt. Gilead Church, as did Ella Carruthers, later Mrs. Oscar Iles, who began her thirty-year career as a Lubbock teacher in 1922. By the fall of 1923, the black people of Lubbock had bought land at 17th Street and Avenue B upon which the school board had built the first black school, a two room building which soon became crowded as the number of potential students grew in the 1920s from less than 20 to 226. In 1929 the school board added another room to the school which had been named by its students in honor of the black poet, Paul Lawrence Dunbar.[14] Five students graduated from the high school level for the first time in 1928, but it included classes only through the tenth grade until 1932 and did not receive accreditation until 1937, considerably later than the white high school. An important leader of black education in Lubbock, E.G. Struggs, began his thirty-five years as principal of Dunbar in 1930. Spurred on by requests and proposals from black leaders, the school board with the aid of federal grants constructed a new four room Dunbar High School at 22nd Street and East Avenue D by 1936. As the number of potential students grew to 488 during the 1930s, classes again overflowed into the black churches of East Lubbock.[15]

The Dunbar Panthers football team organized in 1931 with Charles Sedberry as unofficial coach and second-hand equipment donated from white schools including Texas Technological College. Damon Hill coached all sports at Dunbar from 1938 to 1950, which included several winning seasons.[16]

Those who sought further education beyond the high school level found the nearest black colleges hundreds of miles away in eastern Texas and Oklahoma. To meet that problem black Baptists tried to establish their own junior college in Lubbock during 1940, but failed when their fund drive fell short. Black people in Lubbock's early years faced segregation and discrimination in education as in social and religious life. But they achieved some progress primarily through their own efforts and their frequent requests and reminders to the school board concerning needs.[17]

Despite an increasing level of education, blacks remained unable to vote in Lubbock until the 1940s. The Democratic party, which completely dominated state elections in the 1920s and

1930s, allowed only whites to vote in its primaries where candidates were chosen for state and local offices. As a result few blacks paid the poll tax to vote in fall elections where Democrats generally faced little or no opposition. Then in the spring of 1944 the United States Supreme Court declared the white primary unconstitutional. After unsuccessful requests to the city council for improved services in East Lubbock, Charles Deo of the Colored Chamber of Commerce and Methodist minister T.A. Amos organized the Carver Heights Voters League in April. At the next Democratic primary in July some election judges still tried to exclude blacks, but twenty voted for the first time. In the next city election, during 1946, the number of black voters increased to 200. Yet blacks remained a small percentage of Lubbock voters and all city offices were elected on an at-large basis rather than by geographical areas. Thus twenty years passed before another Methodist minister, the Rev. A.W. Wilson, became the first black to run for a city office, when he lost a city council race in 1964. Despite a variety of voter registration efforts and campaigns by blacks in the 1960s and 1970s, the only successful candidate was Joan Ervin who won a seat on the school board in 1970 and again in 1974. Working outside of elective politics, black leaders during World War II established the Men's Civic Club which founded the Carver Heights Nursery, bought furniture for a school, and contributed to other projects.[18]

Other forms of discrimination fell before decisions by federal courts and laws enacted by Congress in the years following the white primary case as the national civil rights movement focused attention on such problems. Public school desegregation came quietly on a limited basis in the fall of 1955 following the *Brown* decision of the Supreme Court, though most children continued to attend overwhelmingly white or black schools, because of residential segregation and the construction of a new Dunbar High School and Struggs Junior High further to the southeast in the 1950s. Only under pressure from the federal Department of Health, Education, and Welfare through the federal courts did the school board desegregate those schools in 1970 by redrawing their district boundaries. Blacks successfully avoided the loss of traditions and activities connected with former black schools by opposing desegregation plans which called for closing the schools.[19]

Despite the *Sweatt* decision of the Supreme Court in 1950 making it difficult to maintain segregation of public higher education, Texas Technological College—later Texas Tech University—did not admit its first black student, Mrs. Lucille Graves, until the summer of 1961 after she received assistance from the NAACP. Texas Tech integrated its sports programs in 1963 and granted its first degree to a black student, Mrs. Ophelia Moore, in 1964. In 1969 the university hired its first black administrator, George Scott. The following year the university granted its first doctorate to a black graduate student, Hortence W. Dixon, and developed an Ethnic Studies program including courses in black studies. Under pressure from HEW, Texas Tech appointed its first black faculty members in 1972. By the early 1970s black students at the university numbered over 200, but remained only 1 per cent of the student body.[20]

Desegregation of public facilities became extensive in 1963 when seventy-two Lubbock restaurants opened their doors to blacks, and complete after the national Civil Rights Act of 1964. The city council in 1963 created an Interracial Commission and appointed two black policemen, after several years without any. Black protests and a night of scattered rioting in 1971 led to the creation of a city Human Relations Committee the following year.[21]

Change remained more limited in other aspects of life for black people in Lubbock. Blacks participated in the city population boom during the 1940s, as their numbers increased to 6,229 by 1950, or 8.7 per cent of the city's 71,747 people. But the direction of residential growth for blacks remained southeast, between 19th Street on the north and Avenue A on the west. To maintain that segregated pattern, but also to provide new, improved housing, Mayor Murrell Tripp and the city council organized the Southeast Lubbock Development Corporation in 1953, though its board included some black leaders. The corporation promoted the creation of Manhattan Heights, though only 250 lots had sold by 1960 because blacks remained suspicious of a white led project. Higher costs and loan problems also slowed the area's growth.[22]

In 1958 the Lubbock Urban Renewal Agency organized with an initial goal of improving the older black section along Avenue A and 19th Street. Better houses, with new water and sewer facilities, street paving, and new schools and parks resulted from the project. The percentage of Lubbock blacks living in dilapidated housing declined from 39 per cent in 1950 to 7.5 per cent in 1970, while the percentage of black occupied houses without complete plumbing facilities fell from over 50 per cent in 1950 to 5.6 per cent in 1970. Less than 2 per cent of white occupied housing was considered dilapidated or without complete plumbing by 1970. But not all of the original families in the area could afford to move back into the newer, more expensive housing. Some people moved into public housing projects. Over 500 more moved into old buildings taken from the urban renewal site to an area outside the northeastern city limits. The area had only well water, and sanitation problems because of animals raised there by some families gave it the name "Pig City."[23]

During the 1960s and 1970s as black population grew to 10,912, or 7.3 per cent of Lubbock's 149,101 people in 1970. The black residential area expanded to overlap with white and Mexican-American sections in northeast Lubbock. Yet the amount of residential integration in the city remained limited. Twenty-five of the thirty-five census tracts in Lubbock contained less than 1 per cent black population, two other tracts contained 1.7 and 2.3 per cent black population, while two tracts were over 90 per cent black. Thus residential integration seemed limited to six tracts with black population percentages ranging from 4.2 to 59.2 per cent.[24]

Urban renewal also may have limited the growth of black business in Lubbock, for it forced several small shops and stores to move or close while the section was cleared for improvements. One important new service became available to the black community in 1961 with publication of the *Manhattan Heights Times,* a bimonthly black newspaper which later became a weekly and in 1966 changed its name to the *West Texas Times.*[25]

Most black people in Lubbock continued to work as unskilled laborers and domestic servants in the 1960s and 1970s, although the percentage of individuals in professional jobs increased from 1 to 3 per cent from 1950 to 1970. As a part of the federal anti-poverty programs of the late 1960s, a Community Action Agency was created in Lubbock with black participation both as administrators and as clients. Yet about one-third of all black families in the city remained below the poverty level in 1970. To attack the issues of poverty, business development, and related social problems, black leaders tried new approaches in the 1970s. A Progressive Corporation for Minority Groups and an East Lubbock Business Association sought to raise capital for investment in business. A branch of the national Opportunities Industrialization Center offered job training in technical skills. Leaders from several organizations tried to promote unified action through a United Black Coalition.[26]

Black people came to Lubbock seeking opportunities for a better life through jobs which also filled the labor needs of the city's white citizens. Blacks in Lubbock grew in numbers and progressed in status primarily through their own efforts, and organizations, with occasional white assistance, but in spite of considerable white prejudice and discrimination. The legal barriers of segregation fell during the years beginning in 1944, but white attitudes and black economic and residential status changed more slowly because of the historical events and cultural patterns which had shaped them.

NOTES

[1] Jack D. Forbes, "Black Pioneers: The Spanish-Speaking Afroamericans of the Southwest," *Phylon*, XXVII (Fall, 1966), 293; William H. Leckie, *The Buffalo Soldiers: A Narrative of the Negro Cavalry in the West* (Norman, 1967), 101, 157-62; Kenneth W. Porter, *The Negro on the American Frontier* (New York, 1971), 494-522; J. Evetts Haley, *Charles Goodnight, Cowman and Plainsman* (Norman, 1949), 241; Lubbock *Morning Avalanche*, January 28, 1932; U.S. Bureau of the Census, *Eleventh Census of the United States, 1890: Population Statistics*, 785; U.S. Bureau of the Census, *Twelfth Census of the United States, 1900: Population Statistics*, Pt. 1, p. iv.

[2] Lubbock *Avalanche*, January 20, 1910, January 28, 1932; interviews by Robert Foster with Charles Sedberry, April 8, 1969, Mack Jamison, April l0,1969; U.S. Bureau of the Census, *Thirteenth Census of the United States, 1910: Population*, III, 832-33; George P. Rush, "The Formative Years of Lubbock, Texas, 1909-1917" (M.A. thesis, Texas Technological College, 1934).

[3] *U.S. Bureau of the Census of the United States, 1920: Comparison, Charactistics, and Population of Texas*, 1,005; Lubbock *Avalanche*, November 13, 1919.

[4] Lubbock *Morning Avalanche*, February 5, 1920, May 27, September 5, 1925; Lubbock City Commission, Minute Book 3, January 23, 1923, p. 117; City of Lubbock, Ordinance Book 1, p. 185.

[5] Interviews by Robert Foster with Waymon Henry, March 29, April 18, 1969, Oscar Iles, March 24, 1969, Charles Sedberry, April 8, 1969; Lubbock Abstract Company, Abstract Volumes, Wheelock Second Addition; U.S. Bureau of the Census, *Fifteenth Census of the United States, 1930*, III, Pt. 2, p. 973; U.S. Bureau of the Census, *Sixteenth Census of the United States, 1940*, II, Pt. 6, p. 1,008.

[6] Interview by Robert Foster with George Eubank, April 16, 1969; City of Lubbock, Ordinance Book 1, September 23, 1926, October 24, 1929; Lubbock *Morning Avalanche*, August 25, 1922, December 9, 30, 1923, April 5, May 24, 28, June 15, 17, November 22, 1924, May 17, 23, 1925, July 16, November 25, 1926, February 6, 18, 1927.

[7] Lubbock *Avalanche*, January 3, 1922; U.S. Bureau of the Census, *Fifteenth Census of the United States, 1930*, III, Pt. 2, p. 1,043; interviews by Robert Foster with Mrs. Waymon Henry, March 29, 1969, Charles Sedberry, April 8, 1969; Lubbock City Directory, 1935, pp. 423-77.

[8] Lubbock *Morning Avalanche*, November 11, 1933, June 15, October 5, November 17, 1937; Lubbock City Commission, Minutes, September 27, 1934; interviews by Robert Foster with Oscar Iles, March 24, 1969, Charlie Guy, May 2, 1969, Mrs. J.M. Robertson, March 28, 1969; Lawrence L. Graves, ed., *A History of Lubbock* (Lubbock, 1962), 565.

[9] Lubbock *Avalanche-Journal*, January 7, 11, February 1, July 5, 1931, December 11, 1932.

[10] Lubbock *Morning Avalanche*, June 19, 1929, June 19, 1930, January 6, July 10, 1931, June 20, 1933, July 20, November 9, 1934, June 20, 1935, June 19, 1937; interviews by Robert Foster with Vernice Ford, April 15, 1969, A.L. Vaughan, March 25, 1969, H.D. Woods, April 1, 1969; *West Texas Times* (Lubbock), September 4, 25, 1975.

[11] Interviews by Robert Foster with Mrs. Waymon Henry, March 29, 1969, Carlton Priestly, April 9, 1969; Lubbock *Morning Avalanche*, July 26, 1924; Boy Scouts of America, South Plains Council, file 119; *Manhattan Heights Times* (Lubbock), December 26, 1963, June 4, 1964; *West Texas Times* (Lubbock), August 21, 28, 1975.

12. Waymon Henry, "50th Anniversary Memorial, Mt. Gilead Baptist Church," typescript in his possession; *Formal Opening of Carter Chapel Christian Methodist Episcopal Church*, January 12, 1969; *Greater Bethel African Methodist Episcopal Church*, September 19, 1954; *Messiah Presbyterian Church*, 37th Anniversary; *Mount Vernon Methodist Church, Service of Consecration, April 14, 1968*; interviews by Robert Foster with Mrs. Irby Whitfield, May 7, 1969, D.C. Fair, April 28, 1969, Mrs. Waymon Henry, April 18, 1969.

13. Interviews by Robert Foster with Mrs. Waymon Henry, March 29, 1969, Charles Sedberry, April 8, 1969, Oscar Iles, March 24, 1969; Lubbock *Avalanche*, May 15, 1919, June 20, 1920.

14. Lubbock School Board, Minutes, July 13, 1920, September 9, 1922, April 18, November 5, 1923, April 5, 1927; interviews by Robert Foster with Oscar Iles, March 24, 1969, E.C. Struggs, April 11, 1969; Robert L. Foster, "Black Lubbock: A History of Negroes in Lubbock, Texas, to 1940" (M.A. thesis, Texas Tech University, 1974), Appendix 2; *West Texas Times* (Lubbock), July 10, 1975.

15. Lubbock *Avalanche-Journal*, May 13, 1928, September 10, 1933, September 13, 1936; interview by Robert Foster with E.C. Struggs, April 17, 1969; Lubbock School Board, Minutes, May 26, 1931, September 6, 1933, October 10, 29, November 19, 1935.

16. Interviews by Robert Foster with E.C. Struggs, April 11, 1969, Charles Sedberry, April 16, 1969, D.H. Hill, April 21, 1969; *West Texas Times* (Lubbock), July 17, 24, 1975.

17. Graves, *History of Lubbock*, 496.

18. Lubbock *Morning Avalanche*, January 14, April 15, July 22, 23, 1944, April 3, 1946; *Manhattan Heights Times* (Lubbock), February 13, April 9, 1964; *West Texas Times* (Lubbock), January 20, 1966, April 9, 1970, September 18, 1975, February 12, 19, April 1, 8, 1976.

19. Graves, *History of Lubbock*, 440; *West Texas Times* (Lubbock), April 1, 8, 1976.

20. Jane Gilmore Rushing and Kline A. Nall, *Evolution of a University: Texas Tech's First Fifty Years* (Austin, 1975), 122-24; *Manhattan Heights Times* (Lubbock), June 4, 1964; *West Texas Times* (Lubbock), April 20, 1972, February 12, 1976; *Ethic Studies at Texas Tech University*.

21. *Manhattan Heights Times* (Lubbock), September 5, 26, October 10, 1963; *West Texas Times* (Lubbock), June 10, September 16, November 18, 1971.

22. Graves, *History of Lubbock*, 435, 438-39, 575-76, 607.

23. Ibid., 438; *Manhattan Heights Times* (Lubbock), August 1, 1963; U.S. Bureau of the Census, *1970 Census of Housing: Facilities and Estimates of Dilapidated Housing*, 43-45; Barbara Bryan Taylor, "Voluntary Metropolitan Councils: Lubbock's Adaptation to Changing Urban Needs" (M.A. Thesis, Texas Tech University, 1969), 52-54; *South Lubbock Sentinel*, May 23, 1968.

24. U.S. Bureau of the Census, *1970 Census of Population and Housing: Census Tracts*, Lubbock, Texas, 1-3.

25. *Manhattan Heights Times* (Lubbock), August 31, 1962; *West Texas Times* (Lubbock), January 20, 1966.

26. U.S. Bureau of the Census, *1970 Census of Population and Housing: Census Tracts, Lubbock, Texas*, 14; Graves, *History of Lubbock*, 438-39; *West Texas Times* (Lubbock), December 29, 1966, March 23, 1967, December 3, 1970, January 14, May 13, 1971, October 25, 1973.

Edward Struggs and Mae Simmons
Two African American Educators and the Provisions for Black Schools in Lubbock, Texas, 1930–1970

June M. Steele

Two extraordinary African Americans, Edward Struggs and Mae Simmons, taught in the public school system of Lubbock, Texas, from the early 1930s to the 1970s. An examination of their educational backgrounds, their careers as public school educators and administrators, and their observations about racial opportunity provide parallels and contrasts with the history of black higher education and public education in Texas during the mid-twentieth century.

Struggs and Simmons's stories illuminate some disparities between the African American experience in Lubbock and that of blacks in South and East Texas. Analysis of the city's reported history of race relations and statements made by Struggs and

Simmons support a claim that during the years from 1930 to 1970, Lubbock offered better educational opportunities for black students and greater professional opportunities for black educators than many large cities in Texas. Struggs and Simmons, members of the Colored Teachers State Association of Texas, eventually earned master's degrees, witnessed the beginnings of integration in public schools, and described positive career and social lives in Lubbock, where African Americans have remained few in number, relative to other cities in Texas.

In race relations, the city of Lubbock defies classification. In the early days of the town's history, from 1900 to 1925, the founder of the *Lubbock Avalanche*, J.J. Dillard, used the newspaper as a forum for expression of his personal campaign to keep blacks out of Lubbock. But his vehemently anti-black editorials attracted little, if any, response from the community.[1]

Lubbock's first black citizens, migrants from other southern states or from South Texas, accepted residential restrictions, separate schools, churches, and cemeteries as facts of life as late as the 1960s. Yet Struggs, Simmons, and other black professionals claimed no overt racial tensions, and volunteered favorable comparisons between Lubbock and cities in South and East Texas where reputations for strong racist attitudes negatively affected the social and professional lives of African Americans.

Cotton production, which began to dominate South Plains agriculture in the mid-1920s, brought the first African Americans, as migrant farm workers, to Lubbock. Some stayed after the cotton harvests to work in the production sector of the industry or in service jobs as the city grew into a trade center. An estimated sixty-three blacks resided in Lubbock in 1920, rising to over 1,100 by 1930.[2] Increasing numbers of blacks prompted a city ordinance of 1923, to limit the African American residential community to an area south of 19th Street and east of Avenue A. Described as the "least desirable residential neighborhood in the city," the black community found itself bounded by railroad tracks adjacent to warehouses and industrial plants.[3]

A growing community of permanent black residents created a demand for black teachers, some of whom would be recruited from other parts of Texas. Under such circumstances Edward C. Struggs accepted a position as both principal and teacher at the recently founded Dunbar School, a three-room facility located on 17th Street, adjacent to the designated black residential section of town.[4] The school drew its name in honor of a distinguished African American poet of the 1890s, Paul Lawrence Dunbar.[5]

The building that housed Dunbar came from part of an older school, originally built for white students, and was moved to 17th Street from another location. In 1930, the year that Struggs arrived, black enrollment exceeded one hundred. Two other black teachers preceded Struggs: Mrs. Ella Iles and Mr. Wilson.[6]

Struggs described the school conditions during the early 1930s as difficult. The students, mainly from migrant-worker families, left town after the fall cotton harvest. Black families that found permanent work in Lubbock faced harsh living circumstances. Unable to afford frame houses, many purchased vacant lots and built dugouts on them.[7] Black schoolteachers never knew how many of their students would make it through each term, and during the harvest educators expected sporadic daily attendance. In spite of these conditions the black school population continued to increase, and the three classrooms were crowded with as many as forty students each from 1930 to 1933.[8]

Strained economic times of the Great Depression added to difficult school conditions. Struggs recalled that all teachers, black and white, received full paychecks in a timely fashion, but usually failed to exchange them for the full value due to the shortage of cash at the banks. Often teachers would have to take their paychecks to two or three different stores, discounting them at each stop in trade for goods.[9] Struggs confirmed the gap between white and black teacher salaries during the early 1930s in the state of Texas. And he made note of the fact that teaching was not as lucrative as other endeavors were at the time: "I taught boys who would come to school on Monday and had made more money shining shoes in the hotels over the weekend than I would make all week teaching school. Many times I wondered if I was in the wrong profession...."[10]

Emphasizing the continuity of school funding in spite of hard economic times, Struggs praised the city of Lubbock's commitment: "Even though the town had difficulty collecting taxes, it was a priority to keep the schools going."[11] The black community also gave the school support. Lacking a janitor, the teachers kept their own coal stoves lit, and parents and students swept floors, weeded the yard, and occasionally shoveled snow or raked leaves.[12]

The program for black students in Lubbock offered some advantages that were unavailable in other parts of the state. Although Struggs believed that Dunbar was shortchanged in terms of the physical plant (citing the old building and overcrowded classrooms), he praised the Lubbock school board for providing the black and white students with the same textbooks, and he noted : "So many places gave Negro schools leftover, used, outdated textbooks, but it wasn't that way out here. We had the same textbooks that the white schools were using."[13]

In other respects Lubbock lagged slightly behind the rest of Texas. For example, as late as 1930, Dunbar included only the first through the tenth grade. Struggs added the eleventh grade to the curriculum in 1931. High school offerings at Dunbar included math, history, English, and general science, but fell short of the more diverse course offerings at all-white Lubbock High School. White students chose from Latin, Spanish, domestic science, manual training, vocational agriculture, home economics, and orchestra as early as 1923.[14]

Born near Dawson, Texas, in 1909, Mae Simmons was the granddaughter of four ex-slaves. Her paternal grandfather moved to Texas from Tennessee, and eventually acquired enough land to support his children and grandchildren in cotton farming in Navarro County. All of the children participated in the demanding manual labor required in cotton agriculture. Contracting polio at age six drastically changed the course of Mae Simmons's life. The disease left her without the use of her right arm, a condition for which her mother spent years seeking treatment. Simmons remembered traveling to different hospitals throughout Texas, and even to St. Louis, to no avail. Her right arm remained paralyzed. Excused from the physical labor of farm work, she concentrated on learning to read and write.[15]

Simmons remembered first feeling called to the teaching profession when she began helping at Sunday school at age thirteen. She attended elementary school in Dawson, eventually graduating from high school in Wichita Falls, where her parents moved in 1927. Simmons was eligible for assistance from the Texas State Rehabilitation Association for crippled children. The organization paid for her study at Prairie View State Normal and Industrial College, the state teachers' college for black students. Knowing that her parents could not pay the tuition for the remaining two years of study, Simmons accepted a teaching job in a one-room schoolhouse in Henrietta, Texas, twenty miles southeast of Wichita Falls.[16]

African American children from the first through the ninth grades attended the school in Henrietta, and Simmons taught there for four years, describing it as "the best experience I ever had." Because their ages varied so widely each child had to be taught individually, creating, according to Simmons, a truly rewarding, fulfilling encounter.[17]

During her four years in Henrietta, Simmons met her husband, eventually following him to Lubbock, where they married in 1939. For the first four months of her marriage Simmons retained her job near Wichita Falls, traveling back and forth by bus, until her husband asked her to resign.[18]

During her first two years in Lubbock, Simmons served as a substitute teacher at Dunbar, but the black population continued to grow. More teachers were needed, and when Edward Struggs encouraged her to go back to school to complete her bachelor's degree, she took the offer to heart. Gaining the consent of her husband, she headed to Houston College for Negroes (later renamed Texas Southern University), where she finished the remaining two years of her degree in education in only twelve months.[19]

In 1942 Simmons returned to Lubbock and began teaching full-time at Dunbar as a fourth-grade teacher. Simmons encountered the same frustrations with the fluctuating student numbers that had challenged Edward Struggs. The seasonal rhythms of the cotton agricultural industry meant that children had high rates of absenteeism, and frequently left Lubbock before completing the school year. Simmons recognized the particular need for dedicated teachers in the South Plains area: "I attended school in Houston and could have gone to work there. But there was so much work to be done here in Lubbock. The children came from families who needed a lot of help."[20]

Determined to improve themselves and the state of black education in Lubbock, both Struggs and Simmons left Texas briefly during the 1940s to pursue graduate work in other states. As African Americans, they were prohibited from graduate study at Texas universities. Struggs earned a master's degree from the University of Michigan, and Simmons left Lubbock between 1946 and 1947 to earn her master's degree in education from the University of Iowa.[21]

Advanced degrees placed Struggs and Simmons above the vast majority of public school teachers in the nation, and the Gilmer-Aiken laws, expediently applied to black teacher salaries in Lubbock in the early 1950s, further raised morale. Lubbock's black teachers had become accustomed to being treated with the same professional deference that was afforded white teachers. For example, teacher meetings had never been segregated in the Lubbock public school system. From the time Edward Struggs came to Lubbock, the white teachers, members of the Texas State Teachers Association, and the black teachers, members of the Colored Teachers State Association, met regularly together with the Superintendent of Schools. Integrated meetings such as these were unusual in Texas prior to 1963. Edward Struggs stated that "even if a meeting was downtown at a hotel the white and colored teachers would sit together and eat together. Not like other places."[22]

Texas managed to avoid episodes of violence that characterized some southern states in the implementation of school integration, but public opinion demonstrated vehement opposition to the plan in the ensuing decades. Change within the school districts evolved so slowly that it was non-existent in many areas.[23] In East Texas school districts employed a multitude of tactics to avoid all-out integration of public schools. The growing national phenomenon of white-flight to suburbia from core urban neighborhoods struck Texas cities as well, aiding recalcitrant whites in attempts to delay school integration. Black and white children simply attended the schools in their respective neighborhoods. Black children were not kept out of white schools by law, but by the conveniently drawn boundary lines of their districts. Another common tactic to avoid integration, the practice of starting integration in the first-grade, assured that full integration would not be achieved for twelve years. Some schools admitted black and Hispanic students, but kept them in separate classes from white students.[24]

Such ploys led to long court battles between school districts and the federal government. The lawsuits in turn led to the enforcement of busing policies that had negative consequences for white and black families alike.

The city of Lubbock kept pace with the State of Texas in some, but not all of the aforementioned categories. Blacks in Lubbock had long been confined to a residential area located in the east section of the city. By virtue of the residential boundaries for school attendance, black children who were now eligible to attend a white school were excluded by residence. Lubbock joined with other southern communities in building new elementary schools in neutral areas and creating magnet programs in specialized subjects—two other methods of avoiding full-scale integration.

In newspaper articles and published histories of Lubbock citizens claim that the city was one of the first to implement integration of the public schools. In reality Lubbock was among the first to submit plans for desegregation, but had several rejected between 1955 and 1984.

Almost a decade elapsed before the teaching staff integrated in 1964, but black teachers in Lubbock could take heart in the fact that they all retained their jobs. Across the nation, desegregation of the public schools led to a loss of employment for many black administrators and teachers. Texas was cited as the state with the greatest number of displaced black educators. According to Struggs and Simmons, Lubbock's black teachers suffered no job loss during the desegregation period. Although African American teachers in Lubbock retained their jobs, the integration process slowly disrupted the cohesiveness of the black community by eroding its anchor institution, Dunbar High School.[25]

By 1968 Lubbock claimed that forty-seven percent of the black children in the school system attended schools other than the four previously all-black institutions at Dunbar High, Struggs Junior High, Phillis Wheatley Elementary, and Ella Iles Elementary. Representatives from the Office of Civil Rights in Washington, D.C., came to investigate Lubbock's school system in 1969.

Unimpressed with what they judged as "limited crossover," national officials were sharply critical of the neighborhood plan, or residence-based attendance plan that Lubbock schools had implemented for integration.[26]

Clearly, reliance on the neighborhood attendance policy would not bring Lubbock Independent School District into compliance with national standards. All across the nation other school districts began to face alternative plans to deal with desegregation. Ultimately the controversial practice of "busing" or transporting children from their neighborhood schools to schools across town in order to achieve racial balance would be tested in Lubbock.[27]

In August 1970 the Justice Department brought a legal suit against the Texas Education Agency and the Lubbock

Independent School District, alleging that federal funds allocated to Lubbock schools were being distributed in a racially discriminatory way. Based on reports of the Civil Rights Office, Lubbock Independent School District had failed to eliminate its "dual school structure," and by continuing to operate four schools, Dunbar, Struggs, Wheatley, and Iles as primarily black schools, was now in jeopardy of losing its funding and accreditation.[28] "Slow but constant efforts on the part of the Justice Department and the school district" prevented disaster. A temporary solution was found in redrawing the attendance lines at Dunbar High School, increasing white enrollment by 263, and Hispanic enrollment by 82, for the 1970-1971 school year.[29]

Other changes implemented soon after involved Struggs Junior High, which lost its ninth grade and began offering only seventh and eighth grades. The first integrated senior class graduated from Dunbar High School in the spring of 1972. But the 1971-1972 school year brought tragedy and tension. In September 1971, a white student shot and killed a black student on the campus at Dunbar. Many white students who had planned on graduating from Lubbock High were apprehensive and resentful of being forced to attend and graduate from Dunbar. The school year played out without further incident, and students who graduated that year and in the next few years after that, whether black or white, reported positive feelings for the school, and expressed satisfaction with the education that they received there.[30]

Lubbock, Texas, seems an unlikely town for educated African Americans with ties and extended families in other parts of the state to spend their retirement years. In spite of a reputation for West Texas friendliness, Lubbock has a less than sterling record of race relations. A history of segregation in its city cemetery and residential areas, a failed urban renewal project, minimal attempts to comply with the *Brown* decision, and isolated incidents of racial tension and violence as late as 1998 mar the record of a city that prides itself on progressive civic-mindedness.[31]

Edward Struggs admitted to harboring some fear about his move to Lubbock in 1930: "I was apprehensive about coming to West Texas. In fact, I didn't know what it was like. I was afraid that I wasn't going to want to stay here when I came. I was born in South Texas. I found out as soon as I got here that Negroes were treated a lot better here in West Texas than anywhere else. That's the reason I stayed."[32]

Recognizing the tremendous contributions that Edward Struggs made to black education from 1930 to his retirement in 1965, a junior high school was named in his honor in 1971. When desegregation efforts forced the closing of Struggs Junior High in 1978, the school board preserved the honor bestowed upon Struggs by renaming Dunbar High the Dunbar-Struggs Magnet Complex.[33]

Members of Mae Simmons family, specifically her siblings and cousins, lived in parts of East and South Texas, and continually urged her to relocate. But she insisted on staying in Lubbock, eventually becoming the principal at Ella Iles Elementary. Simmons's career in Lubbock extended over thirty years. She retired in 1972, stating problems with her health, particularly regarding her paralyzed arm, as the reason for her retirement. In addition to her thirty years of combined service as classroom teacher and principal in three Lubbock schools, Simmons had volunteered extensively in many civic service groups such as the Lubbock Planning Council, Lubbock Cancer Society, National Polio Foundation, United Way, YWCA, YMCA, Girl Scouts, and Boy Scouts. In 1970 the city of Lubbock dedicated a park and community center to her, a monument to her years of service. The Mae Simmons Community Center, located at 23rd Street and Oak Avenue, hosts many cultural and recreational events. At the park's dedication ceremony in 1970, Mae Simmons humbly responded to the tribute, "Am I worthy of this?"[34]

Over the course of their careers in Lubbock, both Struggs and Simmons took advantage of leaves of absence from the public school system to pursue graduate degrees out-of-state, giving them ample opportunities to seek employment elsewhere. Both returned to the South Plains, expressed job satisfaction and strong beliefs in the availability of professional opportunities in the community, and chose to retire in Lubbock.

The grateful city of Lubbock immortalized two educators through the dedication of Struggs Junior High and Simmons Park. But professional satisfaction derived from desegregated teacher meetings, the swift application of the Gilmer-Aiken laws, and attainment of advanced degrees, perhaps creating an atmosphere of opportunity for black educators of Lubbock in the mid-twentieth century.

NOTES

[1] Lawrence L. Graves, "Government, Finance, and Public Services," in Lawrence L. Graves, ed., *A History of Lubbock: From Town to City* (Lubbock, Tex.: West Texas Museum Association, 1962), 157.

[2] Ibid., 158.

[3] Winfred Steglich, "Population Trends," in Lawrence L. Graves, ed., *A History of Lubbock* (Lubbock, Tex.: West Texas Museum Association, 1962), 438.

[4] Edward C. Struggs, interview by Lynn Musselwhite, February 22, 1969, tape recording, Southwest Collection, Texas Tech University, Lubbock.

[5] Edgar Toppin, *A Biographical History of Blacks in America Since 1528* (New York: David McKay Company, Inc., 1971), 286.

[6] Struggs interview with Musselwhite.

[7] Ibid.

[8] Ibid.

[9] Ibid.

[10] Edward C. Struggs interview with Robert Foster, April 11, 1969, Southwest Collection, Texas Tech University, Lubbock.

[11] Ibid.

[12] Ibid.

[13] Ibid.

[14] Lawrence L. Graves, "Education, Welfare, and Recreation," in Lawrence L. Graves, ed., *A History of Lubbock* (Lubbock, Tex.: West Texas Museum Association, 1962), 533.

[15] Mae Simmons interview with Richard Mason, tape recording, Southwest Collection, Texas Tech University, Lubbock.

[16] Ibid.

[17] Ibid.

[18] Ibid.

[19] Ibid.

[20] Ibid.

[21] Ibid.

[22] Struggs interview with Foster.

[23] Ibid.

[24] Robert A. Calvert and Arnoldo De Leon, *The History of Texas* (Wheeling, Ill.: Harlan Davidson, Inc., 1980), 439.

[25] Struggs interviews with Mussellwhite and Foster; Simmons interview with Mason.

[26] C. Len Ainsworth, "Education and Medicine," in Lawrence L. Graves, ed., *A History of Lubbock* (Lubbock, Tex.: West Texas Museum Association, 1962), 252.

[27] Ibid., 253.

[28] Ibid.

[29] Ibid.

[30] *Lubbock Avalanche-Journal*, January 8, 1991.

[31] Alwyn Barr, *Black Texans: A History of African Americans in Texas, 1528-1995* (Norman: University of Oklahoma Press, 1996), 186.

[32] Struggs interview with Robert Foster.

[33] *Lubbock Avalanche-Journal*, August 8, 1979.

[34] Simmons interview with Mason.

The Beginnings of Integration in San Angelo I.S.D.

Gregory A. Doherty

"We conclude that in the field of public education the doctrine of 'separate but equal' has no place." With those few words Chief Justice Earl Warren struck down the precedent of *Plessy v. Ferguson*, which had legally rationalized segregation of the races since 1896. The 1954 *Brown v. Board of Education of Topeka* decision applied provisions of the Fourteenth Amendment to public education and mandated societal strides toward racial equality. However, the much less heralded "enforcement" decision of May 31, 1955, flung the door wide open for local districts to delay racial integration. Warren, speaking on behalf of a unanimous court, found that "additional time" may be necessary "to carry out the ruling in an effective manner." This ruling gave birth to the "with all deliberate speed" time frame.[1]

While other school districts in the old Confederacy marched toward racial integration with greater deliberation than speed, the Board of Education in San Angelo moved relatively quickly to establish good faith compliance with the high court's edict. As late as 1965 only twenty-five per cent of southern school districts allowed African-American children to attend white schools, and it took the Civil Rights Act of 1964 and subsequent litigation to prod segregated districts to pursue integration more vigorously. In the West Texas town of San Angelo, however, this scenario did not play out. Not only did the school board adopt a policy of incremental desegregation sooner than others, it moved with startling speed. The formation of the desegregation policy in the San Angelo Independent School District, the reason's why the policy developed promptly, and the general reaction of the town to racial integration combined to form an interesting and important piece of the city's history.[2]

A special session of the Board of Trustees of San Angelo I.S.D. met in the Administration Building on July 5, 1955. The agenda of the meeting centered on a single issue: integration. A full complement of trustees gathered in the Board Room to discuss the possibility of racial desegregation with several members of the San Angelo African-American community. Upon request from the Board, C.H. Mims, the principal of the Black schools (Blackshear, Hammond, and Carver), invited L.A. Raibon, District President of the National Association for the Advancement of Colored People (NAACP); Fred B. White, District Secretary of the NAACP; Odell Scott, Parent-Teacher Association President at Hammond Elementary; L.M. Johnson; and N.C. Coffee to present their views to the trustees.[3]

After a brief discussion concerning perceived cultural barriers between Black-American students and their white peers including use of the English language and moral standards, one board member expressed concern that the educational process for whites would be retarded while the schools focused their efforts on equalizing education for the races. Superintendent G.B. Wadzeck's memorandum to the Board stated concern over potential reaction from parents, overcrowding, and discipline problems should the trustees opt for immediate integration. In a list of preliminary desegregation proposals Wadzeck advocated a three year delay in three plans and proposed immediate integration in only one. Wadzeck's initial commitment to prompt integration was admittedly questionable. However, trustee Curt Steib, a San Angelo attorney, worried about possible legal ramifications if desegregation failed to win immediate approval. Dr. W.B. Rountree also urged the Board to act promptly, because he felt stalling incurred greater legal risk.[4]

Raibon, testifying before the school board as a citizen of the community rather than a representative of the NAACP, praised the trustees for their "liberal" inclinations and expressed faith that the Board could "iron the problem out without any conflict of any kind." Assured that the proposed new high school (the current Central High School) would be centrally located in San Angelo and that permissive integration would not be forced upon the African-American students, Raibon left satisfied that the Board's intentions originated in good faith.[5]

Scott, a mother of children at Blackshear High School, said she saw no way that integration could adversely affect the Black community. In fact, Scott claimed that white teachers could teach the children "much better" than Black instructors. Coffee and Johnson generally praised the Board's desire to desegregate and dismissed potential difficulties as minor when compared to the enhanced social and educational opportunities available at the white schools.[6]

Mims testified that discipline problems were inevitable with integration, because Black-Texan children were socialized in an environment where force represented the prime tool of behavioral control. According to Mims, Black students would likely rebel against a white authority figure unless they feared the use of force as punishment. Although assured that his teachers would not lose their jobs after desegregation, Mims still expressed considerable reservations about integration, saying that if given a choice he preferred his child attend "the colored school."[7]

With the 1955-1956 school year looming less than two months away, Board President Frank M. Pool suggested that the trustees adopt a policy rather than a detailed plan. Thus, the historic meeting of the San Angelo school board ended after over three hours of discussion with the adoption of the following resolution:

> In compliance with the ruling of the Supreme Court of the United States, May 17, 1954, and following action by the State Board of Education, the San Angelo Board adopts a policy eliminating segregation in the San Angelo Independent School District. We ask the Administration to work up a three (3) year plan to effect this policy.[8]

Charged with this board mandate, Wadzeck spoke with the various leaders of the Black community in San Angelo and personally interviewed each parent with a child enrolled in any of the top three grades at Blackshear High School. He found that only five of eighty-one students preferred continued segregation. As dusk fell over the Concho Valley the evening of July 26, 1955, Superintendent Wadzeck placed four desegregation proposals before the Board of Education.[9]

Wadzeck's first proposal recommended immediate integration of Blackshear's top three grades at San Angelo High, the reassignment of Mims to duty as an assistant principal and counselor to Black students of San Angelo High, early registration of the African-American students attending their new high school, and rigid school zones for each elementary school. Students residing in a district where their race comprised a minority could request a transfer to another school for a period of only three years. The length of the Board minutes dedicated to this proposal and the thoroughness with which it was presented relative to the other three plans leaves no doubt that the administration hoped that this recommendation would win Board approval.[10]

The second proposal retained the elementary school stipulations but rejected high school integration for three years or until the new high school was constructed. The third proposal recommended a one year study period to determine the best means of desegregating. The final option advocated the rigid elementary school's attendance zones with a transfer option for minority students attending predominantly white schools. But it only allowed high school integration for those students who could demonstrate that they needed classes offered exclusively at San Angelo High.[11]

Only the first proposal contained no option for the trustees to employ the "deliberate speed" excuse to delay racial integration. Three of Wadzeck's proposals included rationalizations embraced by a majority of Southern districts. But the San Angelo trustees claimed no such exemption. A unanimous board (with Alvin Hay abstaining and Rountree absent) voted to adopt the immediate integration of San Angelo High while limiting race-related school transfers to a period of one year. By 10:00 P.M. on July 26, merely two months after the Supreme Court's enforcement decision, San Angelo I.S.D. embraced integration.[12]

In 1955 enrollment studies indicated that approximately 6.5 percent of the 8,154 students in S.A.I.S.D. were African-American. While only sixty-two Black-Texans attended San Angelo High during 1955-1956 school year, the presence of Black students in previously all white classrooms represented a significant departure from the norm of the day. Years later Wadzeck told a Justice Department attorney that neither the school board nor his administration received any petitions or urging to integrate the district in 1955. Thus, desegregation of San Angelo schools appears completely voluntary. Faced with no immediate threat of legal action by the NAACP and provided an excuse for stalling integration in the enforcement decision of the Supreme Court, the San Angelo trustees were under no direct pressure to integrate in 1955. The question persists . . . why did they pursue the course of immediate integration?[13]

Curt Steib claimed that having two attorneys on the Board (himself and Third Court of Appeals Judge Earl Smith) made the trustees more sensitive to legal issues. Steib said, "We told them the writing was on the wall, which way the law was going, and that it was not going to go back." Undoubtedly, the two attorneys knew the magnitude of *Brown*. But equally certain, they recognized that the Warren court provided a gaping window for delay. Whatever the case, both trustees voted for immediate integration in 1955 in the belief that desegregation was justified both legally and morally. In fact, in a September 1, 1955, board meeting, the trustees discussed the real possibility that the district's state funding could be cut-off because of the board's integrationist policy. A phone call was placed to Dr. J.W. Edgar, Commissioner of Education, who informed the trustees that his office had determined that the worst case scenario would be a court order to re-segregate, but that financial harm could come if the district failed to comply with such an order. No less than Gov. Allan Shivers warned local school districts of the possibility of this repercussion. Thus, desegregation could well have been both legally and financially counterproductive if the Texas Supreme Court had ruled favorably on several laws blocking state funds to districts considering integration. With the possibility of the loss of state funds to the San Angelo district, the board's decision to desegregate cannot be dismissed as monetarily Machiavellian.[14]

The "incredible behind the scenes influence" of *San Angelo Standard-Times* owner and publisher Houston Harte cannot be discounted as a factor in the school board's decision to combine the races. Missourian by birth Harte proved to be "a pivotal force around whom San Angelo revolved," and his stature as community leader appears indisputable. Harte's position on desegregation may be viewed in the editorials of the *Standard-Times* which Dean Chenowith, the editorial page editor, penned. As owner/publisher of the paper, Harte exercised omnipotent control over the opinions expressed in the editorials. Carrie E. Greene, a student of African-American education in San Angelo, referenced several editorials as evidence that the *Standard-Times* stood firmly behind the Board's decision and that Harte called citizens to do likewise. Harte's special relationship with Sen. Lyndon Baines Johnson, the foremost advocate for national civil rights legislation, indirectly supports the idea that Harte backed the policy of desegregation. Whether Harte supplied the impetus for the July 5 resolution and subsequent adoption of immediate integration or merely advocated the board's action post facto remains unclear. What is interesting is that in the span of only three weeks, Wadzeck seemed to move from a position advocating delay to one favoring immediate action. Whether his meetings with Blackshear parents or pressure from local elites came to bear upon his opinion remains equally obscure. It is crystal clear that Wadzeck was a relative late-comer to the party favoring immediate integration.[15]

Regardless of the opinions of community leaders and trustees, a smooth transition to racial integration demanded the support of the rank-in-file in San Angelo. According to a special front page article in the *Standard-Times* on July 27, 1955, popular opinion in town ranged from enthusiasm, to resigned acceptance, to hesitance. Acknowledging that a few negative comments reached the newspaper office, the article highlighted the opinions of a cross section of the San Angelo community. An anonymous Black-Texan expressed disappointment with the school board's decision, reasoning that the segregated arrangement had functioned well for years. Joe N. Flores explained that he grew up learning not to deal with African-Americans socially, and he believed that the time was not yet right for racial interaction. Still, the vast majority of the responses mirrored that of Mrs. Arch Lewis, a mother of two school-aged daughters: "I am impressed with the school board in working this thing out so rapidly. It will be good to have all this behind us. People I know with children seem ready for this...."[16]

Integration proceeded throughout the 1955-1956 school year without much hoopla. In fact, Mims' report to the school board in a regularly scheduled meeting on January 17, 1956, represented the only official board discussion of the process of desegregation during the first year. Mims cited a high percentage of failing grades, lack of social participation, and an increased danger of dropouts as the primary problems facing Black-Americans in the newly desegregated high school. Conversely, Wadzeck noted extensive African-American participation in the Student Council, drill team, choir, and athletic team during their first year in San Angelo High School. Only the first football game dance and the homecoming dance segregated the races of San Angelo High.[17]

Busy dealing with lunch-room rioters complaining about an abbreviated lunch hour and the planning of the new high school campus, the San Angelo Board of Education left the future of integration in the hands of Wadzeck's administration. The integration story of S.A.I.S.D. did not conclude on September 1, 1955, with the arrival of sixty-two African-Americans at San Angelo High School, but the opening act had played out on a stage of strong, innovative leadership and general community support.[18]

NOTES

[1.] Loren Miller, "Very Deliberate Speed," in *The Segregation Era, 1863-1954*, eds. Allen Weinstein and Frank Otto Gatell (New York: Oxford University Press, 1970), 285, 287-88.

[2.] Ibid., 288.

[3.] *Minutes of the Board of Education of San Angelo Independent School District*, July 5, 1955, deposited in the San Angelo Independent School District Archives (Hereinafter cited as *Minutes*).

[4.] Ibid., p. 1.

[5.] *San Angelo Standard-Times* (San Angelo, Texas), July 6, 1955, p.1; *Minutes*, July 5, 1955, pp. 1-2.

[6.] *San Angelo Standard-Times*, July 6, 1955, p. 1; *Minutes*, July 5, 1955, p. 2.

[7.] *Minutes*, July 5, 1955, p. 3.

[8.] Ibid., p. 1.

[9.] G.B. Wadzeck, "History of Integration: San Angelo Independent School District," July 20, 1970, p. 2, deposited in the San Angelo I.S.D. archives (Hereinafter cited as "History of Integration"); *San Angelo Standard-Times*, July 27, 1955, p. 1; *Minutes*, July 26, 1955, pp. 1-4.

[10.] *Minutes*, July 26, 1955, pp. 2-3.

[11.] Ibid., pp. 3-4.

[12.] *San Angelo Standard-Times*, July 27, 1955, p. 1.

[13.] *San Angelo Standard-Times*, July 6, 1955, p. 1; *Attendance Zone Charges*, April 30, 1969, p. 3, deposited in the San Angelo I.S.D. archives; "History of Integration," p. 1.

[14.] *San Angelo Standard-Times*, May 17, 1984; *Minutes*, July 26, 1955, p. 2; *Minutes*, September 1, 1955, pp. 1-2; *San Angelo Standard-Times*, July 3, 1955, p. 9.

[15.] Personal interview with Royce Smith, Guidance Counselor for San Angelo Independent School District, June 23, 1992; *The Ram Page*, Angelo State University, San Angelo, Texas, April 14, 1972, p. 3; Carrie E. Greene, "The History of Education Provided for Negroes in San Angelo, Texas, From Inception to Integration, September 1955" (M.A. Thesis, Texas Southern University, 1956), p. 85; *The Ram Page*, April 14, 1972, p. 3.

[16.] *San Angelo Standard-Times*, July 27, 1955, pp. 1-2.

[17.] *Minutes*, January 17, 1956, p. 3; Oral interview with G.B. Wadzeck found in Greene, "The History of Education Provided for Negroes in San Angelo, Texas," Appendix J.

[18.] *San Angelo Standard-Times*, January 21, 1956.

Desegregation in West Texas
The United States v. Ector County I.S.D. Case

Bryan L. Smith

In numerous works, Meyer Weinberg, a noted historian on school integration, shows that the establishment of unitary public education facilities in the nineteen sixties and seventies was not easily accomplished. In most instances, segregated communities offered some resistance to integration. The amount of resistance depended largely on the degree of community (residential, public, and educational) segregation. According to Weinberg, the greater the degree of separation, the greater resistance to integration.[1]

A review of Census Department records for Odessa and Ector County from 1921 to the present reveals an arrant historical pattern of residential segregation among the African American and Mexican American population.[2] Ergo, the state of public education for the two minority groups in Ector County was one of inferior and segregated facilities, a pattern that reflected the status quo of *Plessy v. Ferguson* (1896) and *Cumming v. County Board of Education* (1899). Not until the Supreme Court's 1954 and 1955 *Brown v. Board of Education* decisions did the situation in this West Texas county begin to change. The *Brown I* and *II* decisions had far-reaching implications for the equal rights of minorities in all facets of daily life, from the desegregation of buses to the establishment of unitary public facilities. Its greatest impetus, however, was towards the equalization of school facilities for minorities.[3]

In the Ector County Independent School District (E.C.I.S.D.), *Brown* forced the implementation of a 1955 integration plan in which African American students could take classes at Odessa High School that were not offered at Blackshear, the all-Black school. The situation remained this way until the landmark Civil Rights Act of 1964 forced the federal government to execute its authority and make *Brown* a practical reality.[4]

On August 6, 1965, E.C.I.S.D. received official notification from the United States Department of Health, Education, and Welfare (HEW) that the school district's 1955 integration plan did not comply with the 1964 Act. Negotiations between HEW and E.C.I.S.D. ensued, and shortly afterwards, the two parties reached an agreement which closed Blackshear as a high school, while keeping it as a junior high facility. As a result of the compromise, all senior high students in south Odessa were assigned to the predominantly Anglo (98 per cent) Ector Junior-Senior High School, while the junior high students had a freedom of choice between Blackshear and Ector.[5]

Still, true integration did not take place. Soon after African American students arrived at Ector, "white flight" ensued in the Ector attendance area. By 1968 Ector likewise became a minority campus, consisting of 10 per cent Anglo, 28 per cent African American, and 62 per cent Hispanic. Although Ector became a minority dominant school, E.C.I.S.D. was still technically in compliance with the 1964 Civil Rights Act because the federal government classified Mexican Americans as "whites." As a result of litigation brought against Texas school districts in the nineteen forties and fifties by the League of United Latin American Citizens (LULAC) and the GI Forum (two civil rights groups which fought for Hispanic accommodation and assimilation into the Anglo community), courts found that Mexican Americans were not an identifiable minority group, but rather "other whites." Consequently, instead of being integrated with Anglo facilities, as LULAC and the GI Forum desired, school districts in Texas used Mexican American students as subjects to integrate the racially identifiable African American schools.[6]

By 1968, HEW had issued new directives calling for the termination of zone boundaries producing segregated facilities. E.C.I.S.D., however, held firm to its desegregation proposal based on the earlier 1965 HEW guidelines. On account of the impasse over the interpretation of integration, the United States filed suit in 1970 against E.C.I.S.D. and twenty-five other Texas school districts that still maintained zone boundaries. The litigation between E.C.I.S.D. and the Justice Department was put on hold when the two parties reached a temporary agreement in August 1970. The compromise called for extending the majority-to-minority transfers to all E.C.I.S.D. students. It also integrated the faculty and staff at the southside schools, the bus transportation system as well as all extra-curricular activities. More important, the court order directed the continued negotiations between the Justice Department (DOJ) and E.C.I.S.D. so that an agreement could be reached to eliminate the segregative attendance zones. Nevertheless, the specific stipulations of the agreement appear to have satisfied both the school district and the government, for the mandated negotiations never took place. *The United States v. E.C.I.S.D.* case subsequently became dormant.[7]

Before the implementation of the 1970 court agreement, African American and Mexican American individuals generally staffed the minority schools of south Odessa. Subsequently, racial relations at the schools were congenial. When Anglo teachers and staff arrived at the southside schools as a part of the 1970 court order, however, racial incidents between the students and Anglo faculty and staff erupted. Although the faculty and staff received briefings on appropriate behavior at minority-dominant schools, such instructions occurred only after the 1970 court order. By 1979, the southside schools were populated by racially insensitive Anglo faculty and staff who had to confront an ever-growing hostile minority student population.[8] The subsequent student-faculty confrontations precipitated an investigation by HEW and a new effort on the part of the Justice Department to resurrect the dormant desegregation case against E.C.I.S.D.

The animosity between students and staff turned into confrontation when Mexican American students left their classes to protest the absence of Hispanic finalists in the cheerleader competition. Fifty Mexican American and African American students staged a similar protest at Ector High, demanding an end to what they considered racial discrimination, substandard education, and poor sanitary conditions at their school.[9]

The investigation by HEW's Office for Civil Rights (OCR) involved "extensive fact gathering and included numerous interviews with complainants, complainants' witnesses, E.C.I.S.D. staff, and community contacts." OCR concluded that "the evidence of testimony, data, facts, and the record as a whole substantiated most of the complainants' allegations." Although the evidence did not support allegations of physical abuse of minority students on the part of Hays Elementary principal Thomas Harrison, the educator revealed his bigotry by claiming that there had always been "Mexicans, Niggers, and Whites in the schools." E.C.I.S.D. Superintendent William Holm disputed the charges made by OCR, claiming that an investigation undertaken by the district more accurately reflected the facts in the case.[10]

In the middle of the school district's investigation, John Bell, HEW's Director of Elementary and Secondary Education (Region VI), sent a letter to Federal Judge William Sessions in El Paso claiming that five more complaints had been registered against

E.C.I.S.D. by minority students. One complaint, by Armando Rodriguez, an Ector High senior, alleged that guidance counselors at Ector asked him and two fellow students to retract the statements they gave OCR in April and subsequently have the retractions notarized. The other three complaints were of the "garden variety," claiming discrimination due to race and national origin.[11]

Except for a portion of the Bell Report, all reviews and reports ignored what had always been the key issue, namely, that minority segregation in eight southside schools was occurring due to the 1970 court order allowing neighborhood schools and majority-to-minority transfers. In fact, minority isolation in the southside schools was worse in 1979 than before the 1970 order. The minority percentage of the school population (thus, the degree of segregation) grew at Rusk and Travis Elementaries from 88 per cent to 92 per cent, and 95 per cent to 99.6 per cent respectively. At Ector High School minority representation increased from 86 per cent to 99 per cent during this same period. The most flagrant example, however, was at Zavala Elementary. In the school year immediately preceding the court order, the minority population of the elementary school stood at 81 per cent. Without attracting notice from the school district or the court, the minority population grew to 554 students, or 96 per cent, by the end of the 1978-1979 school year. The data clearly illustrate that during the nineteen seventies, when a court order was in force, students and residents of south Odessa had seen the degree of segregation worsen in E.C.I.S.D.[12]

As a consequence of the OCR report, Richard Epps and Craig Crenshaw, of the Justice Department's General Litigation Section, conducted an on-site investigation in Odessa on November 1979. Subsequently, Epps and Crenshaw notified Superintendent Holm and the board of trustees that E.C.I.S.D. had to "commence to study and develop plans to reduce minority dominance in the southside schools."[13]

In the next six months, Superintendent Holm undertook the task of designing a plan to meet the requirements set forth by the federal attorneys. On May 6, 1980, Holm announced a public hearing for May 15th so the district could air its elementary school desegregation plan. At the meeting the school administration presented the "cluster plan"[14] to the board of trustees and 650 people at Bonham Junior High.[15]

The cluster plan, which involved great logistical planning on the part of E.C.I.S.D., sought to eliminate minority dominant schools by clustering them with Anglo dominant schools on the city's northside. The proposal called for the busing of 8,000 elementary students at a cost of $500,000 in motor fuel alone. One Anglo parent remarked that "there's no way you can guarantee that my child won't be hurt, physically, or psychologically by taking him out of his neighborhood." Another parent showed distaste for the plan by urging the district "to pursue this thing in the courts, because if this thing is adopted, it will really be tough for me to let my boy go to Ector County Public Schools."[16]

On May 28, 1980, the school district held another hearing on the cluster proposal, this time at Ector High School. Unlike the respondents at Bonham, the parents at Ector generally supported the plan. One parent, Dorothy Coleman, reflected the general mood of the crowd noting: "busing isn't the end of the world, not for us, nor for our kids, nor their education." Curtis Norris, howbeit, summed up the skepticism in the southside community: "no one complained about busing as long as it was one way [south to north], now that its both ways—now that white kids will be bused across the tracks in the other direction (south)—people are complaining."[17]

After the hearings, it became apparent the board faced a cluster plan which, rather than resolving the Anglo-minority debate over desegregation, exacerbated the feelings of the community. The southside residents could clearly see that the cluster concept would eliminate the minority dominant schools in their neighborhoods. The northside residents on the other hand, overwhelmingly opposed the cluster idea. They believed, and correctly so, that their children would carry the burden of busing in the cluster plan. Against this background, on June 6, 1980, the board of trustees decided to shelve the cluster proposal.[18]

By the middle of June, Holm decided that a new desegregation initiative should center around the "quality of education, rather than the movement of students." Hence, he and his staff began developing a plan which became known as "Access to Excellence." At the end of the month, the superintendent gave the board of trustees a draft version of the proposal, which they overwhelmingly approved. On August 14, 1980, the plan was made public and formally approved by the board.[19]

The long-awaited desegregation effort by E.C.I.S.D. called for the mixing of racial enrollments at elementary and secondary schools by enticing students to academic specialty schools (Magnet schools) throughout the district. The "Access to Excellence" concept addressed what the school district believed was the "essential question" so frequently articulated by the minority community in Odessa. That is, one that stressed "quality educational opportunities rather than the physical movement of children."[20]

In the larger context, the "Access to Excellence" plan contained flaws. First, Holm and the school district held the impression that the minority community preferred quality education over racial integration. At a public hearing three months earlier however southside residents made it abundantly clear that they preferred busing. Second, although "Access to Excellence" might indeed have resulted in superior curricula, the logic of "quality" over "movement" was a throw-back to the days of racial accommodation and the "separate but equal" principle. Consequently, residents of south Odessa began a campaign to return desegregation back to the "movement" standard.

The two main participants in the fight against "Access to Excellence" were board trustee Vicki Gomez and the Community Redress and Unity Concerning Integration at All Levels, or CRUCIAL, headed by Rev. Laurence Hurd. Gomez initiated the attack on specific aspects of the plan. She charged the concept lacked the ambition necessary to improve reading scores at southside schools (the lowest of all E.C.I.S.D. campuses) and that the minority teacher recruitment plan was "too little, too late." She also objected to the petrochemical instrumentation program at Ector High School, saying that it was "vocationally oriented to prepare non-college bound students for labor in the oil fields."[21]

Laurence Hurd, an African American Baptist minister, attacked the plan not for its content, but for what it failed to do. According to Hurd and CRUCIAL, "Access to Excellence" simply was not designed to integrate E.C.I.S.D. schools. Most members believed the plan represented a stall tactic to keep "desegregation away from Odessa and Ector County for another several years."[22]

On October 3, 1980, the Department of Justice concurred. According to DOJ attorney Richard Epps, the "voluntariness of the plan left school desegregation in E.C.I.S.D. totally to chance with no guarantee that there would be any substantial movement of students." Epps continued by stressing, "because of the well-defined residential segregation in Odessa and the continued drawing of attendance zones around segregated neighborhoods, it is plainly foreseeable that most of the schools in the system would remain grossly segregated in their racial make-up." Lastly, Epps advised E.C.I.S.D. officials that it would be his duty to seek a judicial remedy if the board did not fulfill its constitutional obligations.[23]

Then, on November 14, 1980, the DOJ attorney urged the school board to approve a consent agreement which called for:

(1) a December 15, 1980, deadline for a complete and specific desegregation plan.

(2) a plan which would guarantee that the percentage of Mexican American and African American students would not exceed 50 percent at any one school, and no school would have over 85 percent Anglo enrollment.

(3) a recruitment effort to hire more minority teachers and administrators, such that the number of minority teachers reflect the racial makeup of the E.C.I.S.D. population.[24]

On November 18, in a closed-door session, the board of trustees instructed E.C.I.S.D. attorney Robert Cox not to sign the consent agreement. Instead, Cox outlined several modifications of the "Access to Excellence" proposal which the school board then held in consideration: primarily the closing of Blackshear Junior High, and the downgrading of Ector from a high school to a junior high facility. The plan also relied on changes in school attendance zones of every secondary and elementary school in the district. The public response to this proposal was even more vitriolic than it had been to the previous one. Trustee John Quisenberry announced in January 1981 that this latest version of "Access to Excellence" also fell short of acceptance. As a result, the school board tabled the proposal, thus leaving desegregation in E.C.I.S.D. in limbo.[25]

Since the complaints of racial discrimination and minority isolation first surfaced in the spring of 1979, E.C.I.S.D. had presented three desegregation plans and held nine public hearings, all of which failed to resolve the impasse. By February 1981, not one student or school had been integrated. For all practical purposes, the efforts of E.C.I.S.D. to desegregate its district and carry out its constitutional mandate to eliminate vestiges of a dual school system had failed. As trustee Sam Gipson said, the board just was not able "to bite the bullet."[26]

Because E.C.I.S.D. had failed to develop a community-wide, acceptable desegregation plan, a major new development occurred in the case. On February 5, 1981, the Mexican American Legal Defense and Education Fund (MALDEF) filed suit on behalf of CRUCIAL as plaintiff-intervenor in the eleven year *United States v. E.C.I.S.D.* case. MALDEF did so because it felt that its "client had waited long enough." Thus, CRUCIAL and MALDEF initiated a four-year litigious struggle to desegregate E.C.I.S.D.[27]

On October 19, 1981, the case of *United States v. E.C.I.S.D.* began in federal district court in Midland. Judge Fred Shannon of San Antonio presided over the case at the request of federal Judge Lucius Bunton of Midland-Odessa.[28] The trial contained two phases: adjudication of liability and the consideration of remedies. Determination of liability—ascertaining if E.C.I.S.D. was liable in maintaining a dual school system—consumed most of the two-week trial. Two key questions arose out of liability: whether E.C.I.S.D. had segregated students based on race and whether the school district provided substandard faculty and curricula to the southside schools? At the conclusion of the trial on October 27, 1981, Judge Shannon found the defendant, E.C.I.S.D., liable.[29]

Although Shannon ruled against E.C.I.S.D., he became much more attentive to the remedial concerns of the defendant. He concurred with every proposal agreed upon by the government and E.C.I.S.D. The judge approved not one of the subsequent objections or remedy proposals made by CRUCIAL and MALDEF.

The death knell to CRUCIAL's crusade, however, came when Judge Shannon ordered the closing of Ector High School. After that, CRUCIAL waited idly for a decision by the United States Fifth Circuit Court of Appeals regarding Shannon's order. Although CRUCIAL did get a temporary victory—in the form of an evidenciary hearing before a new judge—from the appellate court, the scope of the ruling all but foreshadowed the outcome.[30] The judges did not object to Shannon's order, and the E.C.I.S.D.-DOJ plan, but did disagree on the manner in which it was attained.

On April 1, 1984, newly appointed Judge Harry Lee Hudspeth of El Paso issued a court order affirming, with some modifications, the E.C.I.S.D.-DOJ plan approved by Judge Shannon. In doing so, he fulfilled the requirements set forth by the Fifth Circuit. Accordingly, the only alternative available for CRUCIAL and MALDEF was to contest the third stipulation of Hudspeth's court order. This provision, which had not been part of any earlier plan and therefore not a part of the appellate review, was the establishment of a tri-ethnic committee.

Hudspeth did not give specific guidelines for the makeup of the panel, only that it be implemented by September 1984, and that it advise the school board and the school administration with respect to the continued execution of the desegregation plan. By April 1984, E.C.I.S.D. submitted a structural document for the advisory group. The school district proposed a committee composed of eleven members: six Anglos, two African Americans, and three Mexican Americans. CRUCIAL and MALDEF proposed an arrangement whereby the three ethnic groups would be represented equally with four members each. On April 22, 1985, after a review of the proposed structures, Hudspeth ruled that both plans failed to please the court. He found that the panel should have an equal number of majority and minority ethnic members, thereby creating a committee of twelve, with six Anglos, four Mexican Americans, and two African Americans members.[31]

As a result of Hudspeth's ruling, MALDEF reduced the number of attorneys involved in the E.C.I.S.D. case. This action by the plaintiff-intervenor brought to an end the litigation over the desegregation of E.C.I.S.D. In line with the court-approved desegregation plan, E.C.I.S.D. supplied CRUCIAL and MALDEF with future reports relevant to the court's supervision of the school district.[32]

A possible explanation for CRUCIAL's decision not to pursue litigation can be found in the first annual report submitted to the court on December 1, 1984. The document shows that as a result of the E.C.I.S.D.-DOJ plan approved by Shannon, desegregation had finally been achieved in Ector County. The report reveals that the total minority populations fell dramatically at all the former minority dominant southside schools. At the elementary level, the magnet programs at Hays, Milam, Zavala, and Travis completely integrated the facilities. Likewise, the closing of Ector High School increased the minority populations at formerly all-white Odessa and Permian High Schools, and the closing reduced the minority population at the newly converted junior high from 99 per cent in 1979 to 48 per cent in 1985.[33]

As a consequence, little remained for CRUCIAL to challenge. All former minority dominant schools were integrated, and former Anglo-dominant schools contained sufficient numbers of minority students. CRUCIAL's continued claim that the closing of Ector High School put an unfair burden on the minority community stood groundless. The plan approved by Judges Shannon and Hudspeth required the forced busing of Anglo students from west Odessa to the Ector facility in south Odessa. Also, the southside elementary magnet schools had sufficient numbers of Anglo children bused from west and north Odessa so that the Anglo population averaged 45 per cent.[34]

CRUCIAL and MALDEF could only legitimize the claim that during the long integrational process minorities in Odessa suffered adversely, for during the fourteen years of litigation the southside students had to endure segregated and inferior educational facilities. But the blame for this fell not on the school district, but on former Texas Attorney General John Ben Sheppard, who through his infamous 1957 suit against the Texas chapter of the NAACP (which created a vacuum in the Texas civil rights movement), took away the main impetus for school desegregation, and caused extended integration-related litigation. This is not to say that Sheppard prevented the NAACP from operating in Odessa, Texas. Rather, his litigation against the group led to chaos and uncertainty in the early civil rights movement throughout the state.[35] Thus, in many parts of Texas, primarily the small urban and rural areas, integration had to wait until the limited resources of the second wave of civil rights activism initiated by the Chicano Movement and *La Raza Unida* Party came to fore. This movement prodded the United States into aggressively pushing for desegregation.[36]

Some might argue that even though no active plaintiff took the lead in the desegregation fight, E.C.I.S.D. still bears the responsibility for maintaining minority dominant schools. It must be remembered, however, that segregation characterized the school system since its establishment. Hence, it was going to take more than HEW guidelines to move E.C.I.S.D. to undertake reforms which the dominant majority of its citizens opposed. Therefore, only vocal organizations like CRUCIAL and MALDEF could prod a reluctant school board and community into action. The case of Ector County exemplifies the finality and convergence of all these factors—the chaos in the early civil rights movement, a prodding federal agency forced to take the litigious lead, a recalcitrant school board and community, and finally, the limited resources of the later Chicano civil rights movement.

NOTES

1. Weinberg wrote four especially good works: *Research on School Desegregation: Review and Prospect* (Chicago: Integrated Education Associates, 1965); *Race and Class: A Legal History of the Neighborhood School* (Washington, D.C.: HEW, U.S. Printing Office, 1967); *Desegregation Research: An Appraisal* (Bloomington, Ind.: Phi Delta Kappa, 1968); and *Integrated Education* (Beverly Hills, Calif.: Glencoe Press, 1968).

2. See Department of Commerce, Bureau of the Census, *Fourteenth Census of the United States, 1920: Population*, Vol. 3, p. 996; *Fifteenth Census of the United States, 1930:* Population, Vol. 3, Part 2, p. 979; *Eighteenth Census of the United States, 1960: Population* (Texas), Vol. 1, Part 45, p. 55, and *Housing*, Vol. 3 (City Blocks), pp. 1-17; *County and City Data Book, A Statistical Abstract Supplement*, 1962, p. 352.

3. Meyer Weinberg, *Minority Students: A Research Appraisal* (Washington, D.C.: National Institute of Education, U.S. Printing Office, March 1977), pp. 17-24.

4. Ector County Independent School District (E.C.I.S.D.), *Board Minutes*, July 14, 1955, notation no. 3401; the *Odessa American* (Odessa, Texas), "Integration Plan In Odessa Rejected," August 6, 1965; "Odessa Integration Plan Studied," August 7, 1965.

5. E.C.I.S.D. *Board Minutes*, June 10, 1965, no. 5445; April 28,1965, no. 5401; May 19,1965, nos. 5421 and 5422; January 7,1966, no. 5563; the *Odessa American*, "School Board Merges Blackshear and Ector," June 11, 1965.

6. Deposition Exhibit Number One, March 19, 1981, *United States v. Ector County Independent School District* (Hereinafter cited as *United States v. E.C.I.S.D.*), case no. MO-70-CA-64 found at National Archives and Records Administration, Southwest Region, Ft. Worth, Texas (NARA); P.L. Griffin, interview by Bryan L. Smith, March 19, 1992; Guadalupe San Miguel, Jr., *"Let All of Them Take Heed": Mexican Americans and the Campaign for Educational Equality in Texas, 1910-1981* (Austin: University of Texas Press, 1987), 177-78; Meyer Weinberg, *The Search For Quality Integrated Education* (Westport, Conn.: Greenwood Press, 1983), 194-230.

7. *Policies On Elementary and Secondary School Compliance With TITLE VI of the Civil Rights Act of 1964* (Washington, D.C.: United States Department of Health, Education, and Welfare, March 1968). The *Odessa American* extensively covered the negotiations and court action, but the citations are too numerous to list here. For a complete account, see, Bryan Lee Smith, "The Desegregation of the Ector County (Odessa) Independent School District, 1965-1985" (M.A. Thesis, The University of Texas-Permian Basin, 1992), notes pages 40-45.

8. Deposition, Floy Hinson, October 13, 1981, *United States v. E.C.I.S.D.*, NARA. At the time of the deposition, Hinson held the position of Director of Special

Populations, and was then a trustee of the board of education. Dorothy Burns, interview by Bryan L. Smith, July 8, 1992, Odessa, Texas.

9. E.C.I.S.D. *Board Minutes*, Executive Session, April 17, 1980, no. 8198; the *Odessa American*, "HEW Launches Probe of E.C.I.S.D. Complaints," April 17, 1979; the *San Angelo Standard-Times* (San Angelo, Texas), "Ector School Probes Continues," April 17, 1979.

10. Harrison quoted in Bell Report, May 17, 1979, located in the *United States v. E.C.I.S.D.* file at the Ector County I.S.D. administration building (E.C.I.S.D.-AB). The board of trustees accepted the administrative review which found the allegations of misconduct on the Part of Mr. Harrison "unfounded." See E.C.I.S.D. *Board Minutes*, July 17, 1979, no. 8261; the *Odessa American*, "Quality of Education Concern Voiced at EHS," August 30, 1979; "Answers Due on School Charges," September 15, 1979; the *San Angelo Standard-Times*, Investigator Probes Complaint," September 5, 1979.

11. Letter, John A. Bell to William S. Sessions, June 28, 1979, NARA.

12. Deposition Exhibits, March 19, 1981, *United States v. E.C.I.S.D.*, NARA; Bell Report, May 17, 1979, E.C.I.S.D.-AB.

13. Letters, Richard J. Epps, Jr., Attorney, General Litigation Section, DOJ, to Robert B. Cox, October 29, 1979, November 22, 1979, November 27, 1979, E.C.I.S.D.-AB; Transcripts, phone conversation between Robert B. Cox and Richard J. Epps, Jr., October 23, 1979, E.C.I.S.D.-AB; E.C.I.S.D. *Board Minutes*, November 20, 1979, no. 8431; Holm quoting Crenshaw and Epps in the *Odessa American*, "Minority Dominance in Southside Schools Rapped," November 16, 1979 (quotation).

14. The concept of clustering schools was a desegregation remedy used by such school districts as Hillsborough County (Tampa), Florida, Pontiac, Michigan; Clark County (Las Vegas), Nevada; and Oxnard, California. See United States Commission on Civil Rights, *School Desegregation in Ten Communities* (Clearinghouse Publication 43), June 1973.

15. Letter, William Holm to Richard J. Epps, Jr., February 6, 1980. In the letter Holm outlined the district's timetable for meeting justice department requirements, E.C.I.S.D.-AB. E.C.I.S.D. *Board Minutes*, May 15, 1980, nos. 8610, 8611, 8612; the *Odessa American*, "Elementary Desegregation Talks Scheduled," May 6, 1980; "E.C.I.S.D. Officials to Air Plans for Desegregation," May 14, 1980; "Desegregation Plan Reactions Are Mixed," May 17, 1980.

16. E.C.I.S.D. Memorandum, "Desegregation Options: Cluster Plan," May 15, 1980, E.C.I.S.D.-AB; E.C.I.S.D. *Board Minutes*, May 15, 1980, no. 8610; Sandy Gettemy (1st quotation), Terry Hoak (2nd quotation), in *Odessa American*, "Desegregation Plan Meets Skeptism [sic] and Concern at Meeting," May 16, 1980; E.C.I.S.D. *Board Minutes*, May 15, 1980, no. 8611.

17. E.C.I.S.D. *Board Minutes*, May 27, 1980, nos. 8639, 8640, 8641; the *Odessa American*, "Pros, Cons Debated at Ector High Busing Meeting," May 28, 1980 (both quotations).

18. E.C.I.S.D. *Board Minutes*, Executive Session, June 6, 1980, no. 8674.

19. Letter, William Holm to Board of Trustees, E.C.I.S.D., June 17,1980, E.C.I.S.D.-AB; E.C.I.S.D. *Board Minutes*, August 12, 1980, no. 8767; August 14, 1980, no. 8774; the *Odessa American*, "Trustees OK 'Access to Excellence' Plan," August 15, 1980.

20. Memorandum, Access-To-Excellence, by William Holm, June 17, 1980 (quotations), E.C.I.S.D.-AB.

21. The *Odessa American*, "Officials Answer Criticism of Desegregation Plan," September 5, 1980.

22. Unidentified CRUCIAL member in the *Odessa American*, "Officials Answer Criticism of Desegregation Plan," September 5, 1980.

23. Letter, Drew S. Days III, Assistant Attorney General, Civil Rights Division, and Richard J. Epps, Jr., to Robert B. Cox, September 30, 1980 (quotations), E.C.I.S.D.-AB; the *Odessa American*, "Ector County Desegregation Plan Nixed," October 4, 1980.

24. Letter, Richard J. Epps, Jr., to Robert B. Cox, November 14, 1980, E.C.I.S.D.-AB.

25. Letters, Robert B. Cox to Richard J. Epps, Jr., November 18, 1980 and November 25, 1980, E.C.I.S.D.-AB; E.C.I.S.D. *Board Minutes*, December 15, 1980, nos. 8946, 8947, 8948, and December 17, 1980, nos. 8951, 8952, 8953; the *San Angelo Standard-Times*, "Ector to Become Junior High," "Ector Plan Similar to Decree," "Elementary Plan Keeps Neighborhood Concept," all articles December 14, 1980, and "Odessa Residents Blast Desegregation Plan," December 17, 1980; the *Odessan*, "Deseg [sic] Plan Draws Fire Over Closing Ector," December 11, 1980; the *Odessa American*, "Odessans Lash Out Against Proposed Busing Plan," December 18, 1980.

26. The *Odessa American*, "Ector High Apparently Will Get A Reprieve," January 29, 1981 (quotation).

27. Letter, Norma V. Solis, Staff Attorney, MALDEF, to Ms. Bobby Pieper, Deputy District Clerk of Court, Midland-Odessa Division, June 18, 1980, NARA; the *Odessa American*, "New Motion Changes Desegregation Suit," February 6, 1981 (quotation).

28. The reluctance of the federal district court to reopen the E.C.I.S.D. desegregation case on its own motion (a district court has that prerogative according to *Manning v. Board of Public Instruction of Hillsborough County*, 1958) might be explained by the fact that between 1970 and 1979 three different federal judges held jurisdiction over the case. In 1974, the original case judge, Ernest Guinn, died. His replacement, William Sessions, then retained control over the case. In 1979, President Jimmy Carter appointed retired E.C.I.S.D. school board trustee Lucius Bunton to the federal bench. He became the first judge to sit in the Midland-Odessa Division for the Western District of Texas. As such, the E.C.I.S.D. case fell within his jurisdiction. As a former defendant in the case, however, Bunton could not preside over it. He likewise did not remove himself from the case until CRUCIAL filed its motion for intervention two years later. Also, during the two-year period he retained jurisdiction, Bunton chose not to reopen the litigation against his former colleagues. Lucius D. Bunton, interview by Bryan L. Smith, June 27, 1992, Midland, Texas.

29. The formal decision of the court on liability came with the court's ruling on the Findings of Fact and Conclusions of Law, April 1, 1982, *United States v. E.C.I.S.D.*, NARA.

30. See, Opinion Of The Court, Randall, Johnson, and Williams, December 29, 1983, *United States v. E.C.I.S.D.* 82-1444, 5th Cir., NARA.

31. Order Of The Court, Harry Lee Hudspeth, March 27 and April 22, 1984, *United States v. E.C.I.S.D.*, NARA; Plaintiff-Intervenors' Request For Reconstitution Of Tri-Ethnic Committee And Suggested Plan For Tri-Ethnic Committee, December 12, 1984, *United States v. E.C.I.S.D.*, NARA; Letter, Robert B. Cox to William Holm, April 18, 1984, E.C.I.S.D.-AB; "News Release," E.C.I.S.D. Communications Department, April 29, 1985, E.C.I.S.D.-AB.

32. Affidavit Of Counsel, Morris J. Baller, April 2, 1985; Court Docket, *United States v. E.C.I.S.D.*, NARA.

33. Annual Report To The Court, December 1, 1984, *United States v. E.C.I.S.D.*, NARA.

34. The figure comes from averaging the Anglo percentages in Table 2, the 1985 column, in Bryan Lee Smith, "The Desegregation of the Ector County (Odessa) Independent School District, 1965-1985" (M.A. Thesis, The University of Texas-Permian Basin, 1992), p. 126.

35. For a complete account, see, Michael Lowery Gillette, "The NAACP In Texas, 1937-1957" (Ph.D. Dissertation, The University of Texas-Austin, 1984), pp. 274-332.

36. San Miguel, *Let All of Them Take Heed;* Jorge C. Rangel and Carlos M. Alcala, "Project Report: De Jure Segregation of Chicanos in Texas Schools," *Harvard Civil Rights-Civil Liberties Law Review*, 7 (March 1972).

CONTRIBUTORS

Alwyn Barr, retired as a Professor of History at Texas Tech University; Barr's scholarly interests include black history, southern history, civil war history, and Texas history. Among his publications is *Black Texans: A History of African Americans in Texas*.

Paul H. Carlson is Professor of History and Director of the Texas Tech Center for the Southwest. An historian of the West and Southwest as well as Native American history, Carlson's many publications include *The Plains Indians* and *Amarillo: The Story of a Western Town*.

Lawrence Clayton was dean of Liberal Arts at Hardin-Simmons University. His many publications focused largely on cowboy life and ranching in the American West. He died in December 2000.

R.C. Crane, one of the founders and a long time leader of the West Texas Historical Association, published widely on West Texas history. He died in January 1956.

Gregory A. Doherty earned his master's degree in history at Angelo State University.

CONTRIBUTORS

Robert L. Foster resides in Austin, Texas. He wrote his Texas Tech master's thesis on the African American community in Lubbock, Texas.

Bruce A. Glasrud is Professor Emeritus of History, California State University, East Bay and retired Dean, School of Arts and Sciences, Sul Ross State University; he currently resides in Seguin, Texas. Glasrud specializes in the history of blacks in the West; he is co-editor of *The African American West: A Century of Short Stories* and of *The African American Experience in Texas*.

Patricia E. Gower currently teaches history at the University of the Incarnate Word. She earned her master's degree at Angelo State University and her Ph.D. at Texas A&M University. When she wrote the article on "Blacks in San Angelo," she was Patricia E. Lamkin.

Tai D. Kreidler received his Ph.D. in history from Texas Tech University. On the staff of the Southwest Collection at Texas Tech, Kreidler also serves as Executive Director of the West Texas Historical Association.

Barbara A. Neal Ledbetter researches and writes on West Texas history. Ledbetter is a public school teacher, and assistant archivist at Fort Belknap. Among her publications is *Fort Belknap Frontier Saga: Indians, Negroes, and Anglo-Americans on the Texas Frontier*.

Donald R. McClung has worked on the career of Lieutenant Flipper. He produced a heavily cited master's thesis at East Texas State University entitled "Henry O. Flipper: The First Negro Officer in the United States Army, 1878-1882" as well as the article in this book.

Bryan L. Smith graduated with a master's degree in history from the University of Texas-Permian Basin, and then attended graduate school at the University of New Mexico.

June M. Steele teaches history at Monterrey High School in Lubbock, Texas; she earned her master's degree at Texas Tech, and continues her research and interest in West Texas history.

Eric Emmerson Strong recently retired from Texas Tech University; for many years he served as head of the Upward Bound program at Texas Tech; he earned a master's degree in history at Texas Tech.

Karen Turner teaches United States history in the Abilene Independent School District.

BIBLIOGRAPHY: WEST TEXAS HISTORICAL ASSOCIATION

***WEST TEXAS HISTORICAL ASSOCIATION YEAR BOOK* ARTICLES ON AFRICAN AMERICANS**

Amin, Julius. "Black Lubbock: 1955 to the Present." *West Texas Historical Association Year Book* 65 (1989): 24-35.

Carlson, Paul H. "William R. Shafter Commanding Black Troops in West Texas." *West Texas Historical Association Year Book* 50 (1974): 104-16.

Christian, Garna L. "Adding On Fort Bliss to Black Military Historiography." *West Texas Historical Association Year Book* 54 (1978): 41-54.

_____. "The Twenty-fifth Regiment at Fort McIntosh: Precursor to Retaliatory Racial Violence." *West Texas Historical Association Year Book* 55 (1979): 149-61.

_____. "Rio Grande City: Prelude to the Brownsville Raid." *West Texas Historical Association Year Book* 57 (1981): 118-32.

Clayton, Lawrence. "Nig London: Throckmorton County Cowman." *West Texas Historical Association Year Book* 67 (1991): 94-100.

Crane, R.C. "D.W. Wallace (80 John): A Negro Cattleman on the Texas Frontier." *West Texas Historical Association Year Book* 28 (1952): 113-18.

Crimmins, Col. Martin L. "Captain Nolan's Lost Troop on the Staked Plains." *West Texas Historical Association Year Book* 10 (October 1934): 68-73.

_____, ed. "Shafter's Explorations in Western Texas, 1875." *West Texas Historical Association Year Book* 9 (October 1933): 82-96.

Doherty, Gregory A. "The Beginnings of Integration in San Angelo I.S.D." *West Texas Historical Association Year Book* 69 (1993): 74-81.

Ewing, Floyd F., Jr. "Origins of Unionist Sentiment on the West Texas Frontier." *West Texas Historical Association Year Book* 32 (1956): 21-29.

_____. "Unionist Sentiment on the Northwest Texas Frontier." *West Texas Historical Association Year Book* 33 (1957): 58-70.

Foster, Robert L., and Alwyn Barr. "Black Lubbock." *West Texas Historical Association Year Book* 54 (1978): 20-31.

Glasrud, Bruce A., and James M. Smallwood. "The Texas Tech School of Black History: An Overview." *West Texas Historical Association Year Book* 82 (2006): 102-19.

Gower, Patricia E. "Blacks in San Angelo: Relations Between Fort Concho and the City, 1875-1889." *West Texas Historical Association Year Book* 66 (1990): 26-37.

Lamkin, Patricia E. (see Patricia E. Gower).

Ledbetter, Barbara A. Neal. "Black and Mexican Slaves in Young County, Texas, 1856-1865." *West Texas Historical Association Year Book* 56 (1980): 100-102.

McClung, Donald R. "Second Lieutenant Henry O. Flipper: A Negro Officer on the West Texas Frontier." *West Texas Historical Association Year Book* 47 (1971): 20-31.

Matthews, James T. "Always in the Vanguard: Patrolling the Texas Frontier with Captain Louis Carpenter and Company H of the Tenth Cavalry." *West Texas Historical Association Year Book* 75 (1999): 110-19.

Miles, Susan. "Fort Concho in 1877." *West Texas Historical Association Year Book* 35 (1959): 29-49.

Pospisil, Jo Ann. "Black Defenders in the American West, 1865 to 1890." *West Texas Historical Association Year Book* 76 (2000): 106-25.

Pruitt, Nicholas. "Broadening the Scope: The High Plains Klan of the 1920s." *West Texas Historical Association Year Book* 82 (2006): 156-69.

Smith, Bryan L. "Desegregation in West Texas: *The United States v. Ector County I.S.D.* Case." *West Texas Historical Association Year Book* 69 (1993): 59-73.

Smith, Ralph A. "Mexican and Anglo-Saxon Traffic in Scalps, Slaves, and Livestock, 1835-1841." *West Texas Historical Association Year Book* 36 (1960): 98-115.

Steele, June M. "Edward Struggs and Mae Simmons: Two African American Educators and the Provisions for Black Schools in Lubbock, Texas, 1930-1970." *West Texas Historical Association Year Book* 77 (2001): 86-98.

Strong, Eric Emmerson. "The Lost Treaty of the Black Seminoles." *West Texas Historical Association Year Book* 75 (1999): 120-30.

Sullivan, Jerry M., ed. "Lieutenant Colonel William R. Shafter's Pecos River Expedition of 1870." *West Texas Historical Association Year Book* 47 (1971): 146-52.

Temple, Frank M. "Discipline and Turmoil in the Tenth U.S. Cavalry." *West Texas Historical Association Year Book* 58 (1982): 103-18.

_____. "Colonel B.H. Grierson's Victorio Campaign." *West Texas Historical Association Year Book* 35 (1959): 99-111.

_____. "Colonel B.H. Grierson's Administration of the District of the Pecos." *West Texas Historical Association Year Book* 38 (1962): 85-96.

Turner, Karen. "Abilene's Minority Population and the 1900 Census." *West Texas Historical Association Year Book* 68 (1992): 113-21.

Williams, Clayton W. "A Threatened Mutiny of Soldiers at Fort Stockton in 1873 Resulted in Penitentiary Sentences of Five to Fifteen Years." *West Texas Historical Association Year Book* 52 (1976): 78-83.

Williams, Mary L. "Empire Building: Colonel Benjamin H. Grierson at Fort Davis, 1882-1885." *West Texas Historical Association Year Book* 61 (1985): 58-73.

INDEX

A Brief History of the Seminole-Negro Indian Scouts, 18
Abilene, Tex., 17, 19-20, 24-25, 98-104
Abilene Colored School, 102
Abilene Copy Shop, 19
Abilene Reporter-News (Abilene), 98
Adams, Hiram, 35
Albany, Tex., 35
Alpha Phi Alpha, 110
Amarillo, Tex., 10, 17-18, 25
American Legion, 110
American Missionary Association, 59
Amos, T.A., 113
Anderson, George, 99
Anderson-Stephenson directory (Abilene), 99
And the Walls Came Tumbling Down, 20
Arthur, Chester A., 67
Asa-Havey, 15
Aston, B.W., 5, 20-21
Atlanta, Ga., 59
Atlanta University, 59
Augur, Gen. C.C., 66
Austin, Tex., 79
Avant, Taylor, 102

Badger, Norman, 74, 76
Baldwin, Theodore, 44, 60
Barr, Alwyn, 24
Barvequero Lake, 35
Beene, Julia Belle Williams, 103
Bell, John, 152
Bell Report, 143
Ben Ficklin, 77
Berger, Charles, 64
Best, Nellie, 93-95
Best, William, 93
Bethel African Methodist Episcopal Church (Lubbock, Tex.), 111
Big Bend, 47-48, 73
The Black Community of Abilene, 19
Blackman, J., 94
Black Rubbers, The (baseball team), 110
Black Seminoles, 84-96
Black Soldiers in Jim Crow Texas, 1899-1917, 18
Blackshear High School (Odessa, Tex.), 141
Blackshear High School (San Angelo, Tex.), 132-34, 137
Blackshear Junior High (Odessa, Tex.), 141, 148
Blakesley, Nate, 20

Bliss, Zenas R., 88
Bonham Junior High (Odessa, Tex.), 145
Booker T. Washington Park (Lubbock), 110
Booker T. Washington Post 808 (Lubbock), 110
Brackettville, Tex., 94-96
Bradley, Beth, 93, 95
Branch, Hettye Wallace, 18
Braun, Matt, 16-17
Breckenridge, Henry, 89, 91-93
Britten, Thomas A., 18
Brooks, J.H., 93-94
Brown, R.A., 42
Brown v. Board of Education, 25, 113, 127, 131, 135, 141
Brownwood, Tex., 34
Bryson, Conrey, 19
Buffalo Soldiers, 23-24, 106
The Buffalo Soldier Tragedy of 1877, 18
Bullis, John L., 52-53, 73, 89
Bullis-Keyes Raid, 52
Bunton, Lucius, 148
Burford, Nathaniel M., 30

Candelaria Mountains, 63
Carlson, Paul H., 17, 20-21, 23
Carmen Mountains, 51
Carpio, P.L., 103
Carruthers, Ella, 111
Carter Chapel Christian Methodist Episcopal Church (Lubbock), 111
Carver Heights Nursery (Lubbock), 113
Carver Heights Voters League (Lubbock), 113
Casas Amarillas, 15
Casas Amarillas Lake, 44
Camp Cooper, 30, 39
Caprock Escarpment, 50
Carpio, P.L., 103
Cefres, Guy, 109
Central High School (San Angelo, Tex.), 154
Chatman, J.A., 109
Chenowitch, Dean, 136
Chihuahua, Mexico, 36, 48
Chihuahua State Militia, 63
Civil Rights Act of 1964, 114, 132, 141
Civil War, 9, 16-17, 22-23, 30, 45, 59, 74, 100, 106
Clairon, John, 35
Clear Fork of the Brazos, 38
Coahuila, Mexico, 51, 87
Coffee, N.C., 132-33

Coffeyville, Kan., 33
Coleman County, Tex., 33
Coleman, Dorothy, 145
Colorado City, Tex., 33
Colorado River, 31
Colored Chamber of Commerce, 113
Colored Relief Association (Lubbock), 110
Colored Teachers State Association of Texas, 120, 124
Community Redress and Unity Concerning Integration at All Levels, 146-51
Concho Weekly Times, 60
Coronado, Francisco, 106
Cotton, 107, 120-22, 124
Cottonwood Street (Abilene, Tex.), 102
Cox, Robert, 148
Crenshaw, Craig, 144
Cross, Mary, 32
Cross, Tom, 32
Cuba, 55
Cumming v. County Board of Education, 141

Daniels, Caesar, 91
Daniels, Charles, 91
Daniels, John, 91
Daniels, Thomas, 91
Dawson, Tex., 122-23
de Coronado, Francisco Vasquez, 17
Del Norte, Tex., 48
Del Rio, Tex., 93, 95
Deo, Charles, 113
Department of the Interior, 90, 92-93
Department of Texas, 45, 49, 66
de Vaca, Cabeza, 17
Diaz, Porfiro, 54
Dillard, J.J., 120
District of the Nueces, 51, 54
Dixon, Hortense W., 114
Dodge, Kan., 33
Doherty, Gregory A., 25
Dortch, Edward, 101
Dr. Lawrence A. Nixon and the White Primary, 19
Dunbar School (Lubbock, Tex.), 112-13, 121-24, 126-28
Dunbar Parent-Teachers Association, 110
Dunbar, Paul Lawrence, 112, 121
Dwyer, Annie, 60
Dwyer, Mollie, 66

Eagle Pass, Tex., 87
Eagle Springs, Tex., 61-62
Eastern Star (Lubbock), 110

East Lubbock Business Association, 116
Ector County I.S.D. (Odessa), 25, 140-55
Ector County, Tex., 140, 147, 150, 152
Ector Junior-Senior High School (Odessa, Tex.), 141, 143-45, 147-51
Edgar, Dr. J.W., 136
Eighth Cavlary, 52
Elkins, G.K., 35
Ella Iles Elementary School (Lubbock, Tex.), 126, 128
Elm Creek (Tex.), 33
Elm Creek Valley (Tex.), 13-14
El Paso, Tex., 17, 19, 143
El Paso Mail Lines Station, 49
El Paso Times (El Paso), 98
Epps, Richard, 144, 147
Ervin, Joan, 113
Estevan, 17

Factor, Pompey, 93
Fayette County, Tex., 32
First Infantry Regiment, 55
FitzPatrick, Elizabeth Ann, 14-15
Flipper, Festus, 59
Flipper, Henry O., 20, 23, 58-67
Flores, Joe, 137
Fort Belknap (Tex.), 14-15, 29-30
Fort Brown (Tex.), 57
Fort Clark (Tex.), 45, 52, 54, 90, 93-94
Fort Concho (Tex.), 24, 45, 60-61, 64, 72-82
Fort Davis (Tex.), 18, 47-49, 58, 61, 63, 65-66, 80
Fort Duncan (Tex.), 88
Fort Elliott (Tex.), 60
Fort Griffin (Tex.), 15, 60
Fort Leaton (Tex.), 51
Fort McKavett (Tex.), 46
Fort Quitman (Tex.), 61-63, 66
Fort Richardson (Tex.), 15
Fort Sill (Ok.), 60
Fort Stockton (Tex.), 49, 61
Fort Sumner (Tex.), 50
Fort Worth, Tex., 43
Frazier, R.T., 41
Freedom on the Border: The Seminole Maroons in Florida, the Indian Territory, Coahuila, and Texas, 88

Galveston, Tex., 78
Gholson, Sam, 32
Gilmer-Aiken Laws, 124, 129
Gipson, Sam, 148
Gober, Francis, 39
Good, John, 35
Gomez, Vicki, 146

INDEX

Gonzales City, 76
Graves, Lucille, 114
Greene, Carrie E., 146
Grierson, Alice, 75
Grierson, Benjamin H., 61-62, 72-74, 76-80
Guo, S., 103

Half Diamond H. Ranch, 33
Halliway, Willis, 35
Hammond School, 132
Hardin-Simmons University (Abilene, Tex.), 20-21
Harrison, Thomas, 143
Harte, Houston, 136-37
Harvey, J.A.S., 102
Haskins, Don, 20
Hay, Alvin, 135
Hays Elementary (Odessa), 150
Hayes, Rutherford B., 52
Henderson, Will, 100-102
Henrietta, Tex., 123
Henry, Waymon, 109
Heyl, Edward M., 46
Hill, Damon, 112
Hillsman, Ada, 100
The History of the Negro, Wichita Falls, Texas, 1880-1982, 19
Hog Creek, 38
Hokey-Pokey ice cream, 102
Holden, William Curry, 21
Hollis, Lawrence W., 100
Holm, William, 143-46
Horse, Chief John, 84, 87, 92
Houston College for Negroes, 124
Hubbard City, 36
Hudspeth, Harry Lee, 149-51
Humphries, Bud, 41
Hunt, Ray, 39
Hurd, Lawrence, 146-47
Hutto, John, 21

Iles, Ella, 121
Iles, Oscar, 111
Indian Territory (Ok.), 15, 60, 87
Inez, Tex., 32
IOA Ranch, 106-107
Iron Mountain, 14
Isaac, Bill, 33

Jackson, Perry, 110
Jefferson, Curley, 91
Jefferson, John, 91, 95-96
Johns, Doke, 101, 103
Johnson, Bob, 110
Johnson, Britton, 13-18, 22-23, 25
Johnson, Earl, 107
Johnson, Lyndon Baines, 136
Johnson, L.M., 132-33
Johnson, Moses (Allen), 13-14, 28
Jones, A.A., 90-91
July, Billy, 91
July, Charles J., 91
July, Fay, 91

Kennamer, L.B., 21
Kent County, Tex., 36
Keyes, Alexander B., 52
Kibbets, George, 91
Kibbets, John, 88, 93, 95
Kincaid, Naomi, 103, 108-109
Knights of Pythias (Lubbock), 110
Ku Klux Klan, 9
Kyle, Bushy, 102

Laguna Plata (Tex.), 15
La Pista de Agua (Tex.), 15
Lampasas County, Tex., 32
Las Moras Creek, Mexico, 52
Laredo, Tex., 51
Lasora Crossing (on the Rio Grande River), 54
League of United Latin American Citizens (LULAC), 142
Leavenworth, J.L., 15
Ledbetter, Barbara A., 22
Leon Hole (Tex.), 49
Lewis, Mrs. Arch, 137
Little Buffalo, 14
Llano Estacado (Tex.), 14, 15, 44, 47, 49
Lock, Wong, 103
London, Nig, 23, 38-43
Loraine, Tex., 36
Lubbock, Tex., 10, 17, 50, 106-16, 119-29
Lucky, Rev. Reuben H., 59
Lynnville, Tenn., 101
Lyons, C.H., 109

Mackanzie, Ranald, 45, 49-50, 54
Mae Simmons Community Center, 128
Maldonado, Juan Manual, 87
Malone, C. Charles, 98-99
Manhattan Heights, 115
Manhattan Heights Times, 116
Mann, Clay, 31, 33-36
Mann, John, 35
Martin, Alec, 33
Matthews, J.A., 39
McCarty, Tom, 77, 79-80
McCline, Millie, 101-102
McDonald, Isaiah H., 48

165

McLaughlen, Napoleon B., 65
McOueen, Lawrence, 102
Mens' Civic Club (Lubbock), 113
Merrill Hotel (Lubbock), 107
Messiah Presbyterian Church (Lubbock), 111
Mexico City, Mexico, 95
Mexican American Legal Defense and Education Fund (MALDEF), 148-51
Midland, Tex., 17, 148
Midwestern State University, 16
Milam Elementary (Odessa), 150
Miles City, Mt., 41
Mims, C.H., 132-34, 137
Minter family (Abilene), 101
Mitchell County, Tex., 23, 31, 36
Mobeetie, Tex., 60
Monahans Sand Hills (Tex.), 47
Moore, Ophelia, 114
Mount Gilead Baptist Church (Lubbock), 111
Mount Vernon Methodist Episcopal Church (Lubbock), 111
Mount Zion Baptist Church (Abilene), 102
Munday, Tex., 43
Musquiz Canyon, Mexico, 61, 87

Nail Ranch (Tex.), 38-39
National Association for the Advancement of Colored People (NAACP), 10, 19, 114, 132-33, 135, 151
National Polio Foundation, 128
Navarro County, Tex., 122
NCAA, 20
Ned, Jim, 32-33
The Negro on the American Frontier, 88
New Deal, 10
The New Handbook of Texas, 17
New York, 50, 77
Ninth United States Cavalry, 93
Nolan County, Tex., 31
Nolan, Nicholas, 60
Nordstrom, Charles E., 66
Norris, Curtis, 145
Notson, William, 74-75
Nueces River, Tex., 47, 51
Nunn, John, 32-33

Odessa, Tex., 17, 25, 140-42, 144, 146-47, 151
Odessa High School (Odessa), 141, 150
Odd Fellows (Lubbock), 110
Office of Civil Rights (Washington, D.C.), 126
Office for Civil Rights (Odessa), 143-44

Oldham, C.E., 33
Oliver, Joel P., 109
Olney, Tex., 43
Opportunities Industrialization Center (Lubbock), 116
Osceola, 92
Our Land Before We Die: The Proud Story of the Seminole Negro, 18
Owens, Laura D., 36

Painted Rock Arroyo (Tex.), 46
Palmer, Talmadge, 39
Palo Duro Canyon (Tex.), 49
Panhandle-Plains Historical Review, 20
Parker County, Tex., 15
Parks, Susan, 28
Pearce family, 100
"Pecos Bill": A Military Biography of William R. Shafter, 18
Pecos River (Tex.), 45-47, 51, 81
Pena Blanca (Tex.), 48
Perdido Creek, 53
Permian High School (Odessa), 150
Perry, Frank, 84, 88, 93, 95
Perryman, Ignacio, 91
Peters colony ranch (Tex.), 13
Phillips, Joseph, 91
Phillis Wheatley Elementary School (Lubbock), 126-27
Piedras Negras (Tex.), 87
Pindar, (Pvt.), 76
Plessy v. Ferguson, 131, 141
Ponder, Ephriam G., 59
Pool, Frank M., 133
Porter, Kenneth W., 88, 95
Powell, Alexander, 94
Prairie View State Normal and Industrial College, 123
Presidio County, Tex., 49
Presidio, Tex., 49
Progressive Corporation for Minority Groups (Lubbock), 116
Public Affairs Press, 20
Pueblo, Co., 41
Punta de Agua, Tex., 15

Quigley, Calvin, 107
Quisenberry, John, 148

Rachel (freedwoman), 29-30
Racial Borders: Black Soldiers along the Rio Grande, 18
Rainey, 35
Raibon, L.A., 132-33
Rattlesnake Springs, 63

INDEX

Reconstruction, 22, 72, 81
Red River (Tex.), 14-15
Remember When? A History of African Americans in Lubbock, Texas, 19
Remo, Joe, 91
Richardson, Rupert Norval, 5, 21
Rio Grande River, 45-47, 51-54, 61-63, 87
Rister, Carl Coke, 21
Rodriguez, Armando, 144
Rodriguez, Innocente, 53
Roosevelt, Franklin D., 10
Rountree, W.B., 133, 135
Rugar, (Mrs.), 103
Rusk Elementary (Odessa), 144

St. Louis, Mo., 123
Salt Creek, 16
Salt Fork (Main Fork) of the Brazos, 49
San Angelo I.S.D. (San Angelo), 25, 131-39
San Angelo *Standard-Times*, 136-37
San Angelo, Tex., 10, 17, 24- 25, 45, 72-83, 131-39
San Antonio *Daily Express* (San Antonio), 76
San Antonio, Tex., 78-79, 81, 148
Sanborn Insurance (Abilene), 99
Sanchez, Antonio, 91
Sanchez, Ray, 20
San Diego River, 53
San Fernado de Rosas, 87
Sand Rock Springs, 33
San Saba, Tex., 78
Santa Rosa Mountains (Mexico), 52, 87, 93-95
San Vicente, 48
Saragosa, 53
Sayles family (Abilene), 101
Sayre, Harold Ray, 18
Scarborough, Mrs. Dallas, 21
Scott, George, 114
Scott, Odell, 132-33
Scurry County (Tex.), 33
The Searchers, 17
Sedberry, Charles, 110, 112
Sedberry, William, 107, 109, 111
Sellers, Nannie Mae, 98-99
Sells, Cato, 91-92
Seminole Indians, 17-18, 22, 24, 73, 84-97
Seminole War of 1835, 92
Senter, Tom, 96
Sessions, William, 143
Seymour, Tex., 40-41
Shackelford County, Tex., 15, 38
Shafter, William R., 17, 23, 44-58, 65
Shannon, Fred, 148-50

Sheffield, Tex., 46
Shelby, (Col.), 94
Sheppard, John Ben, 151
Sheppard, Morris, 91-92
Shields, John, 91, 94
Shivers, Allan, 136
Silver Creek (Tex.), 31, 33
Simmons, Mae, 25, 119-30
Sing, John, 103
Sing, W., 103
Siouan Campaign, 55
Sivad, Doug, 92
Sixteenth United States Infantry, 77
Slaton, Tex., 49, 110
Smear 62 (medicine), 43
Smith, (Dr.), 77
Smith, Berry, 101
Smith, Bryan L., 25
Smith, Earl, 135
Snyder, Tex., 33
Sonora (Mexico), 36
Spain, 9, 17, 40, 86, 106
Spanish-American War, 55, 93
Spear, James, 76
Stafford, Ida, 111
Steele, June M., 25
Steib, Curt, 133, 135
Stephenson, John L., 99-100, 103
Stevenson, Mrs. L.M., 21
Stith, Will, 100
Storrs' School, 59
The Story of "80 John": A Biography of One of the Most Respected Negro Ranchmen in the Old West, 18
Strong, Eric Emmerson, 24, 84
Struggs, Edward G., 25, 112, 119-30
Sun Boy, 15
Swanson, Donald, 95
Syracuse, N.Y., 77

Tankersley, (Mrs.), 79-80
Tankersley hotel, 77, 79-80
Taylor County, Tex., 32
Taylor, Nathaniel, 73
Taylor, Sadie, 111
Tennessee, 13, 28, 101, 122
Tenth United States Cavalry, 52, 58-59, 61, 65, 72-73, 76-77, 80
Terrazas, Joaquin, 63
Texas and Pacific Railway (T&P), 101
Texas A&M University Press, 18
Texas Attorney General, 151
Texas Education Agency, 126
Texas Rangers, 76, 78
Texas Southern University, 124

Texas State Board of Education, 134
Texas State Rehabilitation Association, 123
Texas State Teachers Association, 124
Texas Supreme Court, 136
Texas Tech Southwest Collection, 19
Texas Tech University (Lubbock), 11, 20, 114
Texas Tech University Press, 19
Texas Technological College (Lubbock), 112, 114
Texas Western College, 19
Thirteenth United States Cavalry, 94
Thomas, George H., 29-30
Thomasville, Ga., 59
Throckmorton County, Tex., 23, 38-43
Tinaja de los Palmas, Battle of, 62
Todd, Bruce G., 18
Travis Elementary (Odessa), 144, 150
Tripp, Murrell, 115
Troop 18 (Lubbock), 110
Troop 19 (Lubbock), 110
Tulia: Race, Cocaine, and Corruption in a Small Texas Town, 20
Tulia, Tex., 20
Tuneful Tales, 19
Turner, Karen, 24
Twenty-fifth United States Cavalry, 88
Twenty-fourth United States Infantry Regiment, 44, 65

United Black Coalition (Lubbock), 116
United States Army, 15, 24, 30, 40, 48, 58, 60, 79, 84, 89, 92, 106
United States Department of Health, Education, and Welfare (HEW), 114, 141-43, 151
United States Fifth Circuit Court of Appeals, 149
United States Military Academy (West Point, N.Y.), 23, 58-60, 67
United States Supreme Court, 108, 113-14, 134-35, 141
United States v. E.C.I.S.D., 140-55
United Way (Lubbock), 128
University of Iowa, 124
University of Michigan, 124
Urban Renewal Agency (Lubbock), 115-16

Valle, (Col.), 62
Vernon, Tex., 40, 43
Victoria County, Tex., 32
Victorio (Apache leader), 55, 58, 61-63, 81
Virginia, 101

Wadzeck, G.B., 132-35, 137-38
Waggoner Ranch (Vernon, Tex.), 40
Wagontongue, 18

Wagstaff, J.M., 101
Walker, Beatrice, 19
Wallace, D.W., 23, 31-37
Wallace, Ernest, 21
Warren, Earl, 131
Warrior, Carolino, 91
Warrior, Dub, 96
Warriors of Color, 18
Washington, D.C., 52, 54, 93-94, 126
Washington, Sam, 91
Watkins, William, 77
Watson, Pleas, 76
Wayne, John, 15, 17
Weatherford, Tex., 13
Wedemeyer, William, 74-78, 80, 82
Weinberg, Meyer, 140
West Texas Historical Association, 11, 20-21
West Texas Historical Association Year Book, 10-11, 17, 20-22, 25
West Texas Times, 116
Wetzel, Dan, 20
Wheresoever My People Chance to Dwell: Oral Interviews with African American Women of El Paso, 19
White Elephant Saloon, 80
White, Fred B., 132
White, Jake, 109
Whitesboro, Tex., 33
Who's Who Among Blacks of Abilene, 19
Wichita Falls, Tex., 17, 19, 25, 43, 123
Wiggins, Bernice Love, 19
Wild Cat (Seminole chief), 87
Williams, H.D., 13
Wilson, A.W., 113
Wilson, Billy, 91
Wilson, Charles Emily, 96
Wilson, Isaac, 91
Wilson, J.W., 33
Wilson, William, 91
Wilson, Woodrow, 94
Winchester rifle, 34
Winegarten, Ruthe, 19
Wisconsin, 74
The Wolf and the Buffalo, 18
World War I, 111
World War II, 10, 42, 110, 113
Worth, William J., 86
Wright, George, 39
Wyoming, 33

YMCA (Lubbock), 128
YWCA (Lubbock), 128
Young County, Tex., 13-16, 22, 27-30

Zavala Elementary (Odessa), 144, 150

www.ingramcontent.com/pod-product-compliance
Lightning Source LLC
Chambersburg PA
CBHW030325080526
44584CB00012B/711